Protecting Paradise in the Driftless

HOW THE KICKAPOO VALLEY RESERVE CAME TO BE

Marcy West

LITTLE CREEK PRESS
MINERAL POINT, WISCONSIN

Little Creek Press
5341 Sunny Ridge Road
Mineral Point, WI 53565

ORDERING INFORMATION
Quantity sales. Special discounts are available on quantity purchases by corporations, associations, and others. For details, contact info@littlecreekpress.com

Orders by US trade bookstores and wholesalers.
Please contact Little Creek Press or Ingram for details.

Printed in the United States of America

Cataloging-in-Publication Data
Names: Marcy West, author
Title: Protecting Paradise in the Driftless: How the Kickapoo Valley Reserve Came to Be
Description: Mineral Point, WI Little Creek Press, 2024
Identifiers: LCCN: 2024918417 | ISBN: 978-1-955656-83-2
Classification: NATURE / Environmental Conservation & Protection
POLITICAL SCIENCE / Public Policy / Environmental Policy
HISTORY / United States / State & Local / Midwest
(IA, IL, IN, KS, MI, MN, MO, ND, NE, OH, SD, WI)

Book design by Little Creek Press

Cover photo credit: Marcy West
Interior sketches credit: Ron Johnson, artist and KRMB Chairman for 25 years

Rivers know this: there is no hurry.
We shall get there someday.

—A. A. Milne, *Winnie-the-Pooh*

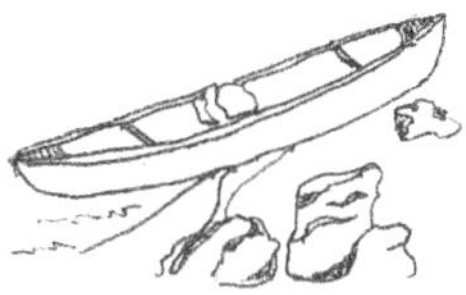

Water does not resist. Water flows. When you plunge your hand into it, all you feel is a caress. Water is not a solid wall, it will not stop you. But water always goes where it wants to go, and nothing in the end can stand against it. Water is patient. Dripping water wears away a stone. Remember that, my child. Remember you are half water. If you can't go through an obstacle, go around it. Water does.

—Margaret Atwood, *The Penelopiad*

Praise for *Protecting Paradise in the Driftless*

The Kickapoo Reserve in western Wisconsin is a gem, and the story of how it came to be is a fascinating tale. From the hurt and pain of a failed dam project that destroyed the local economy to a bipartisan political success story, it is an inspiring tale that reminds us that even bad things can be made whole with the right leadership. Marcy West is the perfect person to tell this story. She helped in the project's creation, nurtured its birth, and led its development, which is considered by all a great success. Her inside knowledge and passion for the project shine through in this great read.

—Brian Rude, former Wisconsin senate president

The story of the genesis of the Kickapoo Valley Reserve is truly vitalizing. It is a story of hope that inspired action and an exemplar of the power of collective imagination when a broad community commits to doing well together. And who better to tell this tale than Marcy West, who has been at the nexus of this effort from the very beginning through the past three decades? We all can learn from her wonderfully told tale.

—Richard L. Cates Jr., farmer and author of *Voices from the Heart of the Land: Rural Stories that Inspire Community* and *A Creek Runs Through This Driftless Land: A Farm Family's Journey Toward a Land Ethic*

The Driftless Area is an ancient landscape with the Kickapoo Valley Reserve lying at its heart. Generations have put their stamp on the land according to values held at their time of tenure. A dam project, proposed to solve one problem, failed to address numerous other considerations. The evolution of public planning processes and the trials and tribulations of consensus-building took decades. Marcy West leads the reader through the success and pitfalls of creating a viable public conservation project. Her passion, empathy, and long-term commitment to the project are inspiring.

—Randy Hoffman, retired DNR ecologist and author of, *Great Nature Wisconsin. A Guide for Nature Immersion in Wisconsin*

Reference Sites of the KVR

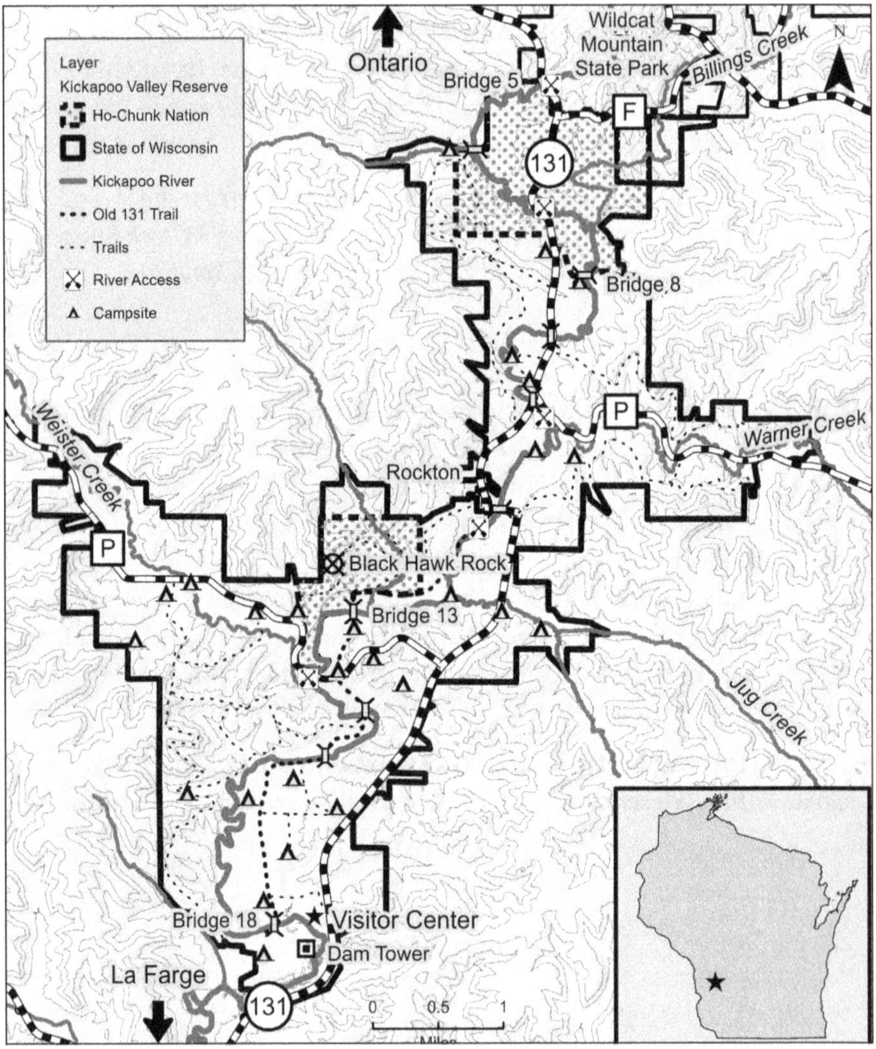

Map: Ben Johnston, GIS and Habitat Restoration Specialist

Contents

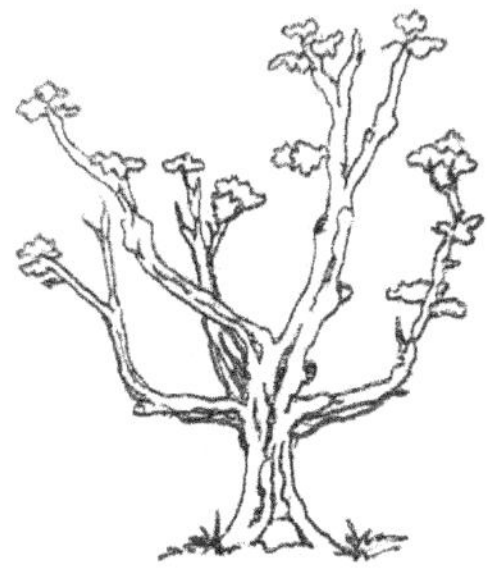

Introduction

In the heart of southwest Wisconsin lies the ecologically diverse Kickapoo Valley Reserve an 8,600-acre publicly protected property and National Natural Landmark, home to more than 400 species of plants and 200 species of birds. Located in the geologic marvel known as the Driftless Area, just beyond the edge of the last glacial retreat, the Reserve's steep terrain is carved by the Kickapoo River. Each year thousands of visitors from Wisconsin and beyond hike its trails, canoe the river, and hunt in its large tracts of forest land. The Reserve is also a unique model for working with sovereign tribes to preserve sensitive environmental and archeological sites.

For many in Wisconsin, it is hard to imagine this land any other way. Yet only some thirty years ago, factors in the creation of the Reserve were being brought together very carefully. The story of its founding, and its success in balancing goals of preservation and recreation, is a testament to cooperation between local citizens, the sovereign Ho-Chunk Indian Nation, elected officials, and the state of Wisconsin. Here in the Kickapoo Valley Reserve (KVR), citizen management proves that those with the most direct link to the land can help heal historic wounds and preserve a piece of paradise at the same time.

The KVR exists today due to a dam project proposed on the Kickapoo River in the late 1960s. The same geological features that make the Kickapoo watershed an ecological and recreational marvel also cause frequent flooding. Elected officials and impacted citizens proposed damming the river to protect downstream communities as early as the 1930s, but the U.S. Army Corps of Engineers (COE) did not begin construction of the La Farge lake and dam until 1969. More than 149 families, businesses, and farms were removed through purchase or by eminent domain. Many landowners believed they were doing the right thing to protect their community from frequent flooding, and they also hoped a lake would bring much-needed tourism dollars to their economically underprivileged region.

Tons of soil and rock were hauled in for the earthen portion of the dam, five miles of State Highway 131 was reconstructed, and a 110-foot water control structure was completed. But in 1975, a combination of factors—cost overruns, increased environmental activism nationwide, recognition of the need to protect archeological sites, and scientific evidence that the project may not meet the intended goal of controlling flooding and improving the tourist economy—made the project untenable. With the dam 70 percent complete, construction was brought to an abrupt halt.

In 1970, Congress enacted the National Environmental Protection Act, which requires that an environmental impact statement (EIS) be prepared regarding proposed federal projects. The timing couldn't have been more consequential. Scientists from the University of Wisconsin in Madison and the Wisconsin Department of Natural Resources (DNR) had previously documented the unique flora and fauna of the area, such as the federal- and state-listed threatened species northern monkshood (*Aconitum noveboracense*) growing out of the rock outcroppings along the river. The variations in land cover and vegetation provided excellent habitat for a wide selection of birds. Over a hundred species of nesting birds were identified on the property, including bald eagles and green herons. Rare birds included red-shouldered hawks, cerulean and Kentucky warblers, Louisiana waterthrushes, and Acadian flycatchers.

The COE submitted an EIS on the La Farge dam in November 1970 that was only ten pages long. Notably absent of details, it was challenged by the Sierra Club and the Natural Resources Defense Council, and the COE was required to respond. The final EIS was expanded to include the environmental and archeological inventories and potential cultural impacts if the dam were to be completed. The EIS served its purpose, as Gaylord Nelson and other politicians paid attention to the scientific information and rescinded their support for the proposed lake. Also contributing to the project's demise were millions of dollars in cost overruns and additional UW research predicting that poor water quality in the forms of phosphorus and nitrogen runoff would result in a shallow, silt-choked lake.

Just as important as the EIS was the relationship with the Ho-Chunk Nation, a sovereign tribe whose ancestors utilized the rivers and woodlands long before the farmers and loggers arrived. As the La Farge lake and dam were being planned in the early 1970s, archeological surveys were also being done. The Wisconsin Historical Society in Madison archived some of the valued artifacts, but most were going to be flooded as there were few laws protecting such sites. Again, timing was everything: the Archeological and Historic Preservation Act, requiring federal projects to mitigate impact to these sites, was signed into law in 1974 and became another reason for the dam project to be stopped.

Sadly, the battle over completing the dam versus ending the project tore the rural community apart. Residents were angry about the loss of property tax revenues when the land shifted from private to federal ownership, the decline in school enrollment as many of the previous landowners moved out of the district, and the fact that their government had made a promise and then broken it. The land sitting idle from 1975 to 1993 didn't help. It was like an open wound that was allowed to fester; the out-of-place, concrete flood control tower and the huge tract of vacant land were visual reminders of the abandoned federal project. Residents watched the land become a dumping ground for everything from old appliances to used motor oil and a playground for people mud bogging in pickup trucks.

Healing eventually came from the citizens themselves. Working with a bipartisan mix of federal and state politicians, a grassroots group of Kickapoo Valley citizens that included town and county board members, business owners, farmers, and self-described "hippies" came up with a proposal that would keep the land in public ownership, have the state pay aids in lieu of taxes, and advocate for the agreed mission statement to "Preserve and protect while enhancing recreation and education." The members of the coalition were adamant that the land should be managed by a board of directors, the majority of whom would reside within the Kickapoo watershed.

What could have been lost by the dam's completion—and how close it came to being lost—is startling. The citizen management model that now oversees this public property may not work everywhere, and by no means has everything gone smoothly. However, right or wrong, the policies were set with good intentions and offered a workable resolution to heal a wound. It will take ongoing vigilance by the Kickapoo Reserve Management Board members, staff, Ho-Chunk Nation officials, and other interested parties to ensure that all they have worked so hard to heal continues to be preserved and protected for future generations.

Prologue

In 1991, my husband, Dave, and I were living in Baraboo, Wisconsin, and we loved it. We had rented an old farmhouse with enough rotting boards to cause perpetual sinus infections, but we had a huge yard and forty acres of woods—our first taste of country life.

Dave was working for the Sauk County Land Conservation Department at the time, and I was commuting most days to my job in Madison as the executive director of what was then called the Wisconsin Land Conservation Association. The WLCA represented all seventy-two counties in the state, so I was on the road a lot for work, but I had never been to the Kickapoo Valley.

I have Jeff Hastings to thank for my first introduction to the area. He was the Vernon County conservationist at the time, and he had organized a canoe trip on the Kickapoo River for area Conservation Department employees, which included Dave's Sauk County crew. Driving the S-curve hill going through Wildcat Mountain State Park on the way to the put-in site reminded me of a family trip from my youth to Vail, Colorado, when I thought for sure my dad was going to hit the guardrail while driving a loaner motor home through a narrow mountain pass west of Denver. Even though the Driftless Area's steep hills are nowhere near as high as the Rocky Mountains, I couldn't believe I was still in Wisconsin as we continued our gorgeous drive through towering white pines, rock outcroppings, and narrow valleys. A quick stop at an overlook gave us an amazing view of our destination.

As our gaggle of conservationists got organized for our trip down the river, Jeff assured everyone that we wouldn't get lost because the bridges are numbered, and the Kickapoo runs north to south. We had to park on the shoulder of the highway because there were no designated access sites at the time, and our group was less than graceful as we slid down the muddy bank to get in the canoes. As we picked up our paddles, the people from the shuttle service casually mentioned that there were some major logjams below Rockton: "So be sure not to miss the takeout at Bridge 10."

As we wound our way down the Kickapoo, Jeff told us we were entering the "government land" that was owned by the federal Corps of Engineers, referred to locally as the Corps (pronounced core). I didn't pay much attention to the rest of his explanation because I was soaking in the splendor of the rock formations and trying to warn Dave about partially submerged logs that could tip us into the river. Despite the muddy banks and the logjams, I was in love.

The beauty of the Kickapoo River stuck with me, and we returned the following spring, when the Virginia bluebells (*Mertensia virginica*) were in full bloom, for a weekend of paddling the river and camping at Wildcat Mountain State Park. Even after all these years and hundreds of trips down this river, the natural beauty of the rock formations, the tree-lined ledges, and the gentleness of the current never cease to amaze me. It's as if Mother Nature stashed a bunch of beautiful things in one spot, intending to come back and take them somewhere else. In the end, she forgot about her hidden treasure, and we get to keep it all.

I am truly fortunate to have been able to play a part in making sure a substantial portion of this river and its adjoining acreage is protected in perpetuity. This is the story of how the KVR came to be.

1
The Headwaters

The winding Kickapoo River has carved its way through layers of rock for millions of years and cut a deep valley into the hilly Driftless Region of southwestern Wisconsin. Beginning as a trickle in Monroe County, near Wilton, the river flows south until it meets the Wisconsin River near Wauzeka in Crawford County. It is the only river to begin and end within the Driftless Region.

Along the way, hundreds of natural springs, creeks, and streams join the main stem. With the corresponding valleys, these tributaries create a dendritic pattern of water reminiscent of intricate tree branches. Adjoining hillsides and ridges support a wonderfully diverse ecosystem of flora and fauna in large tracts where the lumberman's saw didn't cut, and the farmer's plow didn't till. These stands of oak and pine are more than 200 years old and include a mix of hemlock and birch that are usually attributed to northern Wisconsin forests.

Presumed to be named after the nomadic Kickapoo Indians, the river and tribe share the loosely translated Algonquin name of "One who goes here, then there." The river's stream miles are often compared with its geographical length to illustrate how the Kickapoo meanders. The river winds 126 miles from start to finish, while the Kickapoo Valley is roughly half that at 60 miles long, north to south. The current flows in all four directions at least twice within one river mile in the upper section and often doubles back on itself during its twisted route southward.

The Kickapoo is a gentle river under normal conditions. Although the gradient is steeper in the northern reaches, the river drops an average of only three feet per mile for most of its route. The depth varies widely, from a mere six inches near sand-filled curves to more than twelve feet where the river nudges rock outcroppings. Notable for the diversity of its aquatic invertebrates, fish, and amphibians, the Kickapoo is classified by the DNR as a cold-water stream in the upper and middle sub-watersheds and a warm-water stream in the lower watershed. Three of the main cold-water tributaries in the upper watershed—Billings, Warner, and Weister Creeks—host an abundance of stone fly, mayfly, and caddis fly larvae, which require cool, clear, well-oxygenated water to survive, as do the several species of trout found in the larger tributaries and main stem.

In addition to the larger tributaries, natural springs percolate from the ground and seep down the hillsides of the Kickapoo Valley. Rainwater and snowmelt work through the more permeable upper sandstone layer and are squeezed out when they run into the solid limestone layer. At elevations of up to 900 feet, the seeps are vital to supporting vegetation usually found in lowlands, such as scouring rush horsetail, a native vascular plant common in Wisconsin; while the aptly named weeping sandstone visible in the outcroppings along the river, with its nearly constant drip of tears, supports rare plants such as northern monkshood and cliff cudweed.

The Kickapoo's network of flowing water from steep hillsides to narrow valley bottoms created a beautiful, bountiful landscape, and as early as 10,000 BC, humans began to use this river system for transportation, fishing, hunting, trapping, and the harvesting of medicinal plants. The first evidence of the valley being occupied year-round through the use of rock shelters in the winter appeared during the Archaic Tradition (7000 BC to 500 BC). During the Woodland Tradition (500 BC to AD 1500), hunting remained the main food source, although domesticated corn and squash were now being cultivated. This was also the period when the tradition of burying the dead in mounds began, but evidence of this practice is limited in areas of the upper valley, where the sugar maple forests to the west and the deciduous forests to the east were not conducive to large-scale mound building.

Artifacts of pottery and tools were left behind during the Upper Mississippian period (AD 1000 to AD 1650). However, they aren't as abundant as the ones found in village campsites in nearby modern-day La Crosse and Prairie du Chien. The rugged terrain discouraged large settlements and left the Kickapoo Valley to nomadic hunters and gatherers from the Kickapoo, Sioux, Fox, and Ho-Chunk tribes, who hunted or trapped beaver, otter, and mink and harvested the plants and berries along the riverbank. Evidence of their route to ceremonial sites still exists in the marker trees documented on the property. Branches or whole trees that were bent and tied or secured to grow in specific directions pointed the travelers to the tallest rock outcroppings. Many of the featured outcroppings also have petroglyphs or rock art depicting the significance of the site or symbols from specific clans.

European settlers began arriving in the Kickapoo Valley in the early 1800s. The white pine forests attracted lumbermen, who could float the harvested logs to mills downriver to supply lumber for America's building boom. Once the land was cleared of timber, homesteaders began to settle in the area. They were drawn by low prices for cleared land, the area's fertile soil, and the abundant sources of water. Agriculture gradually replaced the logging industry as the primary livelihood for residents of the valley. The initial cultivation of wheat morphed into dairy production along with specialty cash crops like tobacco. Creameries and cheese factories were built up and down the valley, while grist mills and small dams put the flowing water to work in grinding corn, wheat, and other grains. Where hillsides were too steep for crops, cattle and sheep were put out to graze.

But the intense logging and traditional farming practices, combined with the steep slopes and vulnerable soil, led to erosion and sedimentation in the Kickapoo River. The proximity to water that had initially attracted settlers became their undoing when periodic floods ruined crops, roads, homes, and businesses adjacent to the Kickapoo River and its tributaries. Tilling and grazing practices became so detrimental that in 1933 the nearby Coon Creek watershed was designated the first Priority Watershed in the nation by the Soil Erosion Service (now the Natural Resources Conservation

Service). Farmers received incentive payments, seed, and fertilizer along with technical advice to end the practice of tilling up and down the hillsides and overgrazing woodlands. Buffer and contour strips slowed the runoff, stabilized the soil, and filtered some of the sediment out before it reached the creeks and rivers. However, although conservation practices were adopted on farms throughout the region, periodic flooding still plagued the Kickapoo Valley.

The historic flood in August 1935 caused so much damage, from the Village of Wilton at the north end of the watershed to the Village of Wauzeka at the south end, that residents requested federal help to control and prevent future flooding—which, in a way, is the beginning of how the Kickapoo Valley Reserve came to be. True to its name's translation, what was intended to go one way for the residents of the river valley—with a constructed dam to control flooding—went in a different direction over six decades.

2
High Water and High Expectations

As part of President Roosevelt's New Deal initiatives and various Flood Control Acts, the U.S. Army Corps of Engineers (COE) and the U.S. Department of Agriculture were assigned to study flood control in the Kickapoo Valley in 1937. By 1940, the study had resulted in a report recommending a dam be built near the unincorporated village of Rockton to protect downstream communities, but the U.S. entry into World War II on December 7, 1941, put all domestic initiatives on hold nationwide.

After repeated flooding in the Kickapoo Valley—including historic levels in 1951 and 1961—residents again called on their elected leaders for help. Congress authorized the COE to continue to study, plan, and construct a dam north of the village of La Farge. The COE was recognized as the authority for water management throughout the United States. As engineering practices evolved, the locks and dams of the Mississippi River, spill structures, and levees were being built throughout the COE St. Paul District's waterways. With ever-increasing confidence in their ability to control flooding, they revised their plan for the Kickapoo River, expanding the initial purpose of controlling high-water events to a project that included a man-made lake to enhance recreation and economic development to attract tourists. The La Farge Lake and Dam proposal was taking shape with high expectations to control the free-flowing, flood-prone river and provide a boost to a struggling rural economy.

The COE estimated $20 million would be needed to purchase approximately 9,000 acres of land between the villages of Ontario and La Farge for the newly planned lake and to construct the dam and water outflow structures. Referenced as an engineering marvel, the dam would include a 110-foot concrete tower to control water levels with a five-foot tunnel outflow, a half-mile-long soil-and-rock berm to basically hold back the water of the upper Kickapoo and its tributaries, and the purchase of more than 140 parcels of land from residents that would otherwise have been covered with water in creating the lake. Artist renditions depicted the result more as a wide river than the common vision of a lake, but nonetheless, it would have had a swath of surface water. Congress finally approved the funds for this expanded project proposal in 1962, and negotiations for land purchases began in 1965.

Although it was well before my time, shared stories indicate many residents supported the plan to dam the Kickapoo for flood control. Repetitive damage to crops, homes, roads, and businesses was tough to manage. The additional plans for a man-made lake may have met with more skepticism in time. Still, investors were quick to buy land adjacent to what was promised to become a recreational lake because of the potential financial gains of owning and developing property with lake views. Local business owner La Verne Campbell shared a visual description and artist's drawing of a hotel proposed for a beautiful spot just north of La Farge that would have overlooked the lake. And local leaders named the residential development on the north side of the village the "Lakeview Subdivision."

In addition to supporting the idea of flood control, some residents and farmers were relieved to have a buyer for their land during the national recession in the early 1970s or were at an advanced age and feeling ready to move to town. Fair market value was offered through the project budget. However, other landowners were heartbroken by the loss of their homesteads and felt the COE offers were too low, even though they were given options to harvest timber and move or reclaim what they could from their buildings. And given the fact the COE was purchasing low-lying land along the tributaries that was usually tilled, some landowners would be left with a house and barn but no land to farm. A few who refused to sell saw their land acquired through the federal authority of eminent domain, taking private land for public use with payment at a set value.

The impact on the community was equally dramatic. Student enrollment dropped. Local municipalities could not reliably collect taxes from the COE as those appropriations were dependent on congressional approval. Lifelong neighbors were separated when they moved away to find better jobs. Many of the people who remained in the area had to adjust to a whole new way of life. James Daines, a former landowner I came to know and respect, offered a shared sentiment that they felt like they were doing it for the good of the community; the flood control and promise of an improved economy were worth the sacrifices individually if it benefited their neighbors and the region.

Even though Congress had approved funding and the property buyouts were proceeding, concerns about the project had been brewing since the early 1960s. As the lake was being planned, archaeologists were called on to survey for significant sites, and they documented evidence of Native American camps, petroglyphs, and artifacts throughout the proposed project area. Some of the most significant finds were cataloged and stored at the Wisconsin State Historical Society since everyone assumed the area would one day be inundated with water.

The proposed lake had also captured the attention of UW–Madison scientists, who recorded an impressive inventory of the valley's plants and animals. In 1971, Hugh Iltis, a professor of botany, composed a thorough document titled "Report on a Canoe Trip Down the Kickapoo River from Bridge 5 to Bridge 18." He cataloged fifty-one individual sandstone cliffs adjoining the Kickapoo River and emphasized the significance of rare plants such as the subarctic primrose, saxifrage, and northern monkshood that grew on and around these rock formations. His report on the plant life in the Kickapoo Valley is still referenced whenever the Reserve's flora and fauna inventory is updated.

With his knowledge of the ecological treasures being threatened by the proposed lake, Professor Iltis became a vocal opponent of the dam project. His letters to the editor arguing against damming the river and creating a lake in the Kickapoo Valley ran in both the *Milwaukee Sentinel* and the *Wisconsin State Journal*, and he also wrote to elected officials and the U.S. Army Corps of Engineers.

As the environmental movement of the early 1970s spread throughout the country, the La Farge Lake and Dam project attracted more scrutiny, and the 1970 Federal Environmental Protection Act required the COE to prepare an environmental impact statement that was one of the first of its kind in the nation. (See further EIS details in Chapter 5.) One can imagine the conflict between two federal acts, since the earlier Flood Control Act of 1936 and revisions to it in 1944 put the COE in charge of multidimensional construction projects to control flooding and offer recreation opportunities, while the environmental movement required them to forecast the impacts of those exact projects. Catastrophic dam failures in various parts of the country added to the scrutiny as flood events proved, from Buffalo to the Mississippi basin, that too many variables in rain amounts, storm tracks, and structural integrity made it impossible to guarantee protection from floods. In some instances, dams made it worse, as berms and concrete walls holding back water burst with higher-intensity storms.

A 1970 article in the *Atlantic* outlined the changing attitudes toward the corps and its water control projects:

> Few politicians publicly criticize the Corps, because almost all of them want something from it at some point—a dam, a harbor, a flood-control project....The overwhelming majority of Corps projects are attractive federal bonuses, given free of charge to communities.... "They take care of all of the states," said one Senate aide, "if there's water in a faucet in one of them, they'll go in there and build a dam."...There is no question that the civil works program of the U.S Army Corps of Engineers, viewed over its long history, has benefited the country. It has made waterways navigable and provided hydroelectric power and flood control. Communities to which it has brought help have been genuinely grateful. Now, however, it is a prime example of a bureaucracy that is outliving its rationale, and that is what is getting it into trouble. As the Corps, impelled by bureaucratic momentum and political accommodation, has gone about its damming and dredging and "straightening" of rivers and streams, it

> has brought down upon itself the wrath of more and more people disturbed about the effects on the environment.[1]

By this time, the scenic Kickapoo River had become increasingly popular with canoeists and outdoor enthusiasts, some of whom were members of the Madison chapter of the Sierra Club and the Citizens Natural Resources Association. Professor Iltis's expertise was referenced in a lawsuit filed by the Sierra Club that forced the COE to rewrite the project's initial EIS. The project gained more statewide and national exposure when reporters began writing articles and opinion pieces about the dam's inevitable impact on the river that many readers had visited over the years.

To complicate matters further, the COE had already exceeded the original cost estimate by millions of dollars, and the project was only partially completed. The University of Wisconsin-Madison was contracted to study the project in relation to water quality and concluded that the lake would be shallow, filled with sediment from the adjacent slopes, and nutrient heavy from farm runoff and human impacts. The final report indicated that the man-made lake would be choked with weeds, which would require continuous maintenance—hardly the recreational attraction the COE had promised.

In a 2017 interview with Dr. Dennis Keeney, one of the UW authors of the environmental analysis of the expected water quality for the proposed lake, he told me, "It felt like being a funeral director relaying the death of the project. With no way to improve septic systems or prevent agricultural runoff, [the lake] would have been a shallow, stinky mess of rotting weeds at the peak of summer."

Local lore about the demise of the project from the majority who supported the promise of flood control and recreation via the construction of a dam could lead you to believe that it was a "damn flower" or a "stupid snail"—the bird's-eye primrose and the cherrystone drop snail—that brought the dam and lake project to a halt. Those are unique species that need the shaded cliffs to survive and, therefore, were highlighted on the rare and endangered lists, but they were only one component in halting work on the project.

What I came to understand was how a combination of issues worked against the project's viability. The COE was nearly $10 million

---

1 Dam Outrage: The story of the Army Engineers by Elizabeth B. Drew, Atlantic Magazine April 1970, https://cdn.theatlantic.com/media/archives/1970/04/225-/413267367.pdf

over budget, and construction wasn't complete; the environmental concerns were well documented and had the public's attention; and there were serious scientific doubts about the structure's ability to control floods or what the water quality of the proposed lake would be. Together, these factors eventually led elected officials who had previously supported the project to oppose it. Congress withdrew funding in 1975, which stopped the construction. The Kickapoo Valley was left with an unfinished dam berm, an abandoned concrete water control tower, almost 9,000 vacant acres, and a string of communities still vulnerable to disastrous flooding.

A great deal has been written about the demise of the La Farge lake and dam. Some sources are more credible and well-researched than others. For those interested in learning more details, I recommend reading *That Dam History: The Story of the La Farge Dam Project*, by Brad Steinmetz, and *The People Remember...: An Oral History of the La Farge Lake and Dam Project*, edited by Bonnie Sterling.

James Daines and I had multiple conversations about those years of stress and heartbreak for many in the community. I didn't live it, so I feel inadequate trying to describe it from their vantage point. Clearly, the way the COE employees had treated the landowners festered as well. For example, James choked up when he told the portion of his story decades later, in 2000, to high school students involved in the oral history project *The People Remember*:

> When they came in to buy it, they used us dirty. I had 120 acres there and was as good a farm as there was. Good rich soil. And he [a representative from the COE] offered me $18,000 for it. I had a good big house... a new garage, tobacco shed, and big barn. Of course, I bucked. I wouldn't sell. So, they'd come back and offer me a little bit more. They said either I sell it or they was going to condemn it. When they condemn it, they said, "We're going back to the first price"—just $18,000. That's all were going to give you.
>
> So they scared us. They were educated dealers. They had all the cards and we didn't have no way to fight 'em.[2]

2 The People Remember...An Oral History of the Kickapoo La Farge Dam Project, Edited by Bonnie Sterling, 2004.

I would often tell James that if I could, I would have turned back time for them so they wouldn't have to go through it. As the years passed, James would attend special events and stop by my office to give recommendations on a variety of tasks, including where I should have the field crew mow in preparation for his family reunions at Potts Corner. He was always polite and full of humor and charm. His grandchildren attended some of the education programs and field trips, which helped him feel better about what the land had become. James passed away in 2014 at the age of 93. Fortunately, his voice and story were recorded as part of the oral history project.

3

Let the Current Do the Work

Following the halt of the dam construction in 1975, various entities tried to restart the project or proposed alternatives, such as a dry dam or smaller check dams on the tributaries. None of these options gained any traction. When the cost of a proposal was compared with the benefits it could provide, the U.S. Army Corps of Engineers (COE) and Congress lost interest. The $28 million already spent on the project was apparently the federal government's limit. Residents of the area who had thought they were doing right for their community by selling land for the good of the project were beyond frustrated that the flood control options were abandoned.

At the same time, residents and communities adjacent to the Kickapoo River were still enduring repeated flooding, which gave those who supported the dam a reason to advocate for its completion in order to protect themselves. Entrenched in their support of man-made control, it was probably hard to imagine alternatives offered through federal programs. For example, the downstream village of Soldiers Grove—twenty-six miles south of La Farge—opted for a federally supported alternative that moved residents and Main Street businesses to higher ground—and in response to the energy crisis of 1978, the new buildings utilized solar power. The move would prove to be a wise decision. In the years since relocating, their village has experienced significantly less damage.

Meanwhile, the nearly 9,000 idle acres of land purchased or secured via easement by the COE became known as the "government land." The federal budget had appropriated few dollars for the property to be managed or patrolled, and the nearest U.S. Army Corps of Engineers staff was more than an hour away in La Crescent, Minnesota. Some fields continued to be leased for agricultural use, further frustrating former landowners who now had to pay to farm what many of them considered to be their land. Residents repeatedly suggested that they wanted to buy their land back, but that wasn't possible since the COE had purchased it with public funds. The land would have had to be offered through a public sale with no guarantee that the former landowners would be the highest bidders.

Mary Bufton was one of the first former landowners I met. She often reflected on the hardest part of the whole saga. As she described her route into town from her home on 24 Valley Road, heading east to County Road P and down Highway 131, she said, "It was a wound allowed to fester [for nearly twenty years] as we watched our neighbors' homesteads be overrun with weeds and the land sit idle. In spring we see lilacs and tulips blooming where the home gardens used to be. It breaks my heart."

They were promised flood control for the good of the community, only to witness the construction start and stop, with no plan for what was to come next, leaving behind a mess for these small communities.

As word spread about a large tract of vacant land with very little oversight, a variety of people started to treat the land as if it were their own. Horseback riders established trails through the hills and valleys. Drivers of all-terrain vehicles and off-road trucks also loved the scenery and utilized the former farm field roads to get to the interior, presumably attracted by the challenge of the terrain and the freedom to go where they wanted. Canoers and campers continued to utilize the river, with canoe rental and shuttle service business owners taking it upon themselves to cut or pull the frequent tree falls so their customers could paddle safely through the logjams on the river.

Time to Move On

By the late 1980s, a group of residents had had enough. They wanted a resolution to this state of limbo that provided little economic benefit to the area and continued to be a blight on their community. Local villages and town and county governments were frustrated that the COE was not a dependable taxpayer. A system known as payment in lieu of tax for federally owned lands came through erratically due to the congressional and COE budget process and was based on a flat fee per acre instead of on the land's actual value.

State Senator Brian Rude and Assemblyman DuWayne Johnsrud and their staffs began collaborating with the residents to come up with an alternative. Even those who had been strong advocates for the La Farge Lake and Dam project were realizing it would never be completed. Brian Rude recalled that the final straw seemed to be when the Wisconsin attorney general rejected a lawsuit by the Vernon County Board on behalf of residents. The suit to force the completion of the dam had previously failed in circuit court, which had ruled the U.S. Army Corps of Engineers had not officially deauthorized the dam and, therefore, could possibly finish it at some point.

Publicity surrounding that lawsuit led two state newspapers to feature opinion pieces on why the dam project was still a bad idea environmentally. Coincidentally, though unrelated, the Wisconsin DNR produced a report in relation to Wildcat Mountain State Park promotions, documenting the Kickapoo River as a tourism attraction for canoers. Vernon County had spent nearly $40,000 on attorneys' fees and hearings—a significant amount for one of the poorest counties in the state in the 1980s. When State Attorney General Donald Hanaway considered the suit and reviewed the reports and analyses in 1987, his lack of interest in litigating sent a clear message that the local governments shouldn't waste any more time or money on the dam and lake project. Dubbed a "boondoggle" in his dismissal, the label seemed appropriate given the federal and local costs, the abandoned concrete tower and partially constructed berm, and the promises made and broken.

Tommy Thompson had been elected Wisconsin's governor in 1986. As a former assemblyman who had represented a neighboring district for twenty years and a self-described "boy from Elroy," Thompson was familiar with the trials and tribulations of the La Farge Lake and

Dam project through both federal and state perspectives. He worked with Senator Rude and Representative Johnsrud to initiate a process to get the land out of limbo by forming a citizen advisory committee that was directed to focus on the future of the chronically ailing economy of the Kickapoo Valley, which included addressing the issues with the failed dam project because its stagnation impacted the entire region. After reviewing all the research, reports, lawsuits, negative media attention, and constituent interests, Governor Thompson and the elected officials familiar with the boondoggle recognized the need for a different approach.

The University of Wisconsin Extension Service was a trusted government entity that operated at the local level in each county. From supporting 4-H programs to helping organize county fairs, the county extension board and staff were active, important, and trusted members of their communities. In 1988, Dr. Ayse Somersan was appointed the dean of the Wisconsin Cooperative Extension. Born in Istanbul, Turkey, she earned a PhD in international economics, and because she had become a leader in rural issues during her career at UW–Madison, Governor Thompson collaborated with her to give the Wisconsin Cooperative Extension an important role in settling the dam project.[3]

Dr. Somersan offered Al Anderson a special two-year position to guide the Kickapoo Valley planning process. Al was a longtime community resource and development agent for the Extension Service. He said that before deciding to accept the position, he did some direct research. He left his house in Baraboo, roughly an hour east of the project area, at four o'clock in the morning to have breakfast in Wonewoc and spend the rest of the day driving along

3 Ayse had a significant impact on my approach to dealing with the project. She had such a positive attitude and served as a mentor to me and countless others dealing with rural issues through the years. An article commemorating her referenced this after her passing in 2017: "[S]he impressed on them [students and colleagues] the importance of having an open mind and learning to lead." (Gloria Hafemeister, "UW-Extension Leader Remembered," *Wisconsin State Farmer*, December 14, 2017, https://www.wisfarmer.com/story/news/2017/12/14/uw-extension-leader-remembered/925701001/.) And she surrounded herself with people who shared that philosophy.

the Kickapoo River, stopping in small towns to talk to people about anything and everything. The shared sense of loss and impact on the entire valley stuck with him. But he also heard throughout the visit from people who were ready to work toward a resolution.

Thankfully, he accepted the project position. Al's quiet demeanor, experience, and understanding of rural issues, combined with the knowledge that the governor, state legislators, and the university now cared enough to pay attention to the Kickapoo Valley and its failed dam project, gave residents hope that a solution could be reached.

At the federal level, Senators Russ Feingold and Herb Kohl and Congressmen Steve Gunderson, Tom Petri, and Dave Obey also felt there needed to be a resolution to the truncated project, as they heard about it repeatedly from constituents, Governor Thompson, and local officials. Despite their different political party affiliations, they would eventually share the responsibility for getting the dam deauthorized, directing the transfer of the land, and securing funding for each aspect of the process through Congress and the state legislature. Regular communications between the elected officials and staff at all levels would prove vital as progress continued.

Al Anderson started in 1991 by convening a group of citizens who came to be known as the Citizen Advisory Committee. Each community up and down the river was invited to send a representative from the local village, town, or school boards. Experts were brought in through the UW system to study economic development and the potential for tourism dollars specific to rural areas.

The Citizen Advisory Committee meetings were held monthly through April 1993. All the meetings were open to the public, and everyone who attended was asked to join the group at the meeting table rather than being seated in the background. Every good facilitator knows simple gestures like this are imperative for successful outcomes, and participants indicated they felt someone was finally listening to them. Al Anderson said the initial meetings had the feeling of a group therapy session as people shared their frustrations over what they'd been through and their hope that their suggestions would finally be taken seriously with this new process. Al recalls one especially poignant statement from a participant: "They told us we were doing this [selling their land] for the public good, and the good didn't come."

A subset of the committee met more frequently and served as

the Drafting Committee to work on the wording of the proposal that would eventually become legislation. Al brought it all together and made sure all the Citizen Advisory Committee members agreed the wording reflected their wishes for the future of the former lake and dam property that locals referred to as their own "9,000-acre backyard."

In 1993, the Citizen Advisory Committee introduced the proposal recommending that the land remain public property open to low-impact recreation. The land was to be protected as a nature reserve, not a preserve. This terminology represents an important compromise between what some viewed as an environmental extreme—protecting every plant and animal with a preserve—and the other extreme of opening the land up to off-road vehicles and building a manufactured amusement park. Whereas a reserve was interpreted as something set apart for a particular purpose; environmentally protected yet open to the public. Al Anderson explained it to me this way: "They didn't want another Wisconsin Dells with fudge shops and man-made water parks. They knew the Kickapoo River and surrounding valleys had a natural beauty that many would enjoy."

The Citizen Advisory Committee also agreed on other important aspects. Reaching a consensus to keep the land in public ownership was easy since residents had become used to open access for nearly twenty years while it was in federal ownership. *How* to keep the land public was more of a challenge, according to various members of the committee. Way back in 1975, when the dam construction was halted, Senator Gaylord Nelson had proposed a riverway park to be administered through the National Park Service. The national riverway park was denied as it did not meet the criteria for national park or scenic waterway status. Residents did not want the land to be administered through the DNR because many believed—rightly or wrongly—that the agency had worked to undermine the completion of the dam and lake project, and they wanted it to be different than a state park.

As the idea of locally based citizen management evolved, the Department of Administration and later the Department of Tourism were identified as logical choices to accept the land on behalf of the state of Wisconsin and develop opportunities for low-impact tourism and outdoor education. But the committee also recommended the land be managed by a board of directors, primarily made up of citizens from the valley, who would have the authority to set policy, hire staff, raise funds, and make payments to local units of government to make up for the lost revenue from property taxes.

Vital to the process were the efforts made to gather support from all the entities affected by the establishment of a publicly owned nature reserve. Members of the Citizen Advisory Committee and Al Anderson met with organizations and municipalities throughout the area to ask for formal resolutions supporting the proposal. State and regional entities were also provided with copies of the proposal and were invited to comment or ask questions.

The proposal was met with overwhelming support at every level. George Nettum, who would become a founding board member for the Reserve, admitted that as a then county board member from Viroqua who had been in favor of the dam, he had to grit his teeth and vote in favor of the resolution. "We had to show the communities that it was time to move on and this was a good alternative because it came from the people who live there," George said.

The proposal was converted into draft legislation with the help of the Wisconsin Legislative Reference Bureau, the Wisconsin Legislative Council, and their lead staffer, Mark Patronsky. I had known Mark for years through my jobs in Madison, and he said the legislation practically wrote itself because the local committee—with Al Anderson's help—had done such a good job putting the proposal together. Of course, having the political muscle of Governor Tommy Thompson, State Senator Brian Rude, and State Representative DuWayne Johnsrud on board helped move the process along.

State Senate Bill 721 and Assembly Bill 349 were introduced in January 1994. A public hearing on the proposed legislation was held in La Farge and attracted more than ninety people, which is a large crowd in such a small community. The local town, village, school, and county boards, which had first heard about the proposal from Citizen Advisory Committee members just fourteen months prior, provided resolutions and letters in support of the bills.

Bill 721 passed in the state senate on March 24 and was reconciled with AB 349 to pass the assembly unchanged on March 25, 1994. Governor Tommy Thompson held the signing ceremony in the La Farge High School gym on April 16 for the residents to witness, and the Kickapoo Reserve Management Board was officially established within the Wisconsin State Statute.

While in the neighborhood, Governor Thompson was interested in seeing the former dam site and concrete tower for himself. Local resident David Mick, who operated a canoe business and a nearby farm, offered to show him around after the ceremony. David is a great storyteller and gladly shared with me that the governor jumped in the canoe shuttle van with him and told his security detail to follow them. The site of the dam is maybe a mile from the school, but somehow, the officers missed the turn on the gravel road leading up to the berm of the partially completed dam. “Imagine those young bucks realizing they had lost the governor somewhere in the Kickapoo Valley. Tommy and I had a good laugh, watching the squad cars look for us from the top of the dam. *That* was a good day!”

The Board’s Inception

Wisconsin State Statute 41.41 created the Kickapoo Reserve Management Board (KRMB) and formalized the objective of the original advisory committee’s proposal:

> The board shall manage land in the Kickapoo valley reserve to preserve and enhance its unique environmental, scenic and cultural features, to provide facilities for the use and enjoyment of visitors to the reserve and to promote the reserve as a destination for vacationing and recreation.

Governor Thompson quickly appointed nine members to the board, which was composed of six locally nominated residents of the valley and three representatives selected by the governor to represent education, tourism, and environmental interests, as outlined in the new statute. In recognition of the local animosity toward the DNR, the board was attached to the newly created Wisconsin Department of Tourism for administrative support, which also provided some hope for an enhanced economic impact from tourists for the valley.

The statutory language listed the powers of the Kickapoo Reserve Management Board as well as the restrictions to that authority. The statute guided the process for management by documenting the “policy-making” role of the board and the delegation of administration to the executive director, establishing the ability to generate revenues, directing payments in lieu of taxes for local municipalities, complying and working with local units of government, and granting law enforcement capabilities. The primary restriction was the inability to sell the land.

At the federal level, in roughly the same time span, Congressmen Steve Gunderson and Tom Petri sponsored language in the Water Resources Development Act of 1994 (H.R. 4460 103rd Congress) to formally deauthorize the La Farge Dam project—which would make it official that the dam would never be built—and direct the land be transferred to the state of Wisconsin. Although the behemoth bill passed in the House of Representatives, it died at the committee level in the senate for issues unrelated to the La Farge project. Progress on the transfer would take another proverbial spin through an eddy before it came out the other side in the 1996 Water Resources Development Act, with a historic directive to co-manage the public land with the Ho-Chunk Nation.

Reconnecting the Ho-Chunk Nation

To better understand Native Americans' interest in the establishment of the Reserve, we must go back some 200 years. The Ho-Chunk people were formally recognized by the U.S. government as inhabiting the region north of Prairie du Chien, Wisconsin, by a series of treaties that started in 1825. However, the Ho-Chunk presence in the area is documented as far back as the 1600s. Depending on the historical period of interest, Sioux, Fox, and Kickapoo tribes also utilized the resources in the region, but for the purposes of this writing, I focus on the history of the Ho-Chunk Nation and encourage interested readers to research the vast collection of writings on Indigenous American history.

The heartbreaking descriptions of the tribe's being displaced by European settlers in this region have their beginnings in the lead rush of the 1820s when miners defied U.S. law and illegally seized Ho-Chunk land in southwest Wisconsin. But what happened during the signing of the 1837 treaty is what I came to recognize as one exceptionally painful example in our history that was rooted in a lack of trust for tribal leaders in negotiations with government entities. After three attempts to remove the tribe from the area, the federal government tricked a young delegation of tribal members into going to Washington, D.C., with promises of supplies for the winter, then threatened these representatives with death if they did not sign the treaty that gave up the rights to their ancestral land. The deceitful practices and broken promises of the federal government in the 1800s would directly affect the modern-day negotiations over the Kickapoo Valley Reserve.

Al Anderson invited Ho-Chunk Nation representatives to the Citizen Advisory Committee meetings during the drafting process. According to others in attendance, representatives for the tribe would attend meetings but were cautious in participating. They did not speak to the issues being discussed but requested copies of draft proposals. Even a professional facilitator like Al Anderson couldn't draw out their opinions or positions.

In 1994, representatives of the Ho-Chunk Nation contacted the Bureau of Indian Affairs (BIA) and the Wisconsin congressional delegation to indicate their interest in the entire property since it was a part of their ancestral lands. Previously completed archeological surveys, increased revenue from casinos, and sovereign nation status, with federal laws validating their role in all federal projects, brought a new dynamic to the efforts to resolve the property status. Since Congress had not specifically appropriated funds for the project for nearly ten years, a case could be made for the land to be transferred to another federal agency, as dictated by the federal surplus-property procedures. The Department of the Interior, where the BIA is housed, is experienced in managing large tracts of land through the Bureau of Land Management and could have advocated for the entire 8,600 acres to be transferred to the Ho-Chunk Nation and held in trust.

Through negotiations with the state's elected officials, a compromise was reached with Ho-Chunk Nation President Chloris Lowe Jr. Twelve hundred acres would be transferred to the BIA in trust for the Ho-Chunk Nation, which would share management responsibility for the entire property with the state of Wisconsin through the KRMB. In addition, a memorandum of understanding between the state and Nation would be required prior to ownership transfer to ensure all archeological sites would be protected, and future land management responsibilities would be outlined in writing with approval by the tribe and state.

Former Congressman Steve Gunderson's notes to Senator Rude at the time indicated the Ho-Chunk Nation's cooperation was based on many things:

> First, people like Chloris Lowe [Jr.] had brought a real sense of professional management to the business of the nation.... As you know, they have a lot going on in terms of the business of the tribe. So, they sought to be good partners in these conversations, as part of a much larger desire to be good partners in all that they do.

The directive for the La Farge Lake project was included (again) in the federal Water Resources Development Act (WRDA), which was passed in 1996. WRDA gave the U.S. Army Corps of Engineers their marching orders on projects nationwide. For the La Farge project, the COE was directed to complete safety modifications to the water control tower, deauthorize the dam and lake project, clean up the worst of the waste sites, resolve any remaining boundary disputes, and complete the relocation of State Highway 131 and County Highways P and F.

Unlike the language in WRDA 1994, the new language included specifications in the acreage: roughly 7,400 acres to the state of Wisconsin and 1,200 acres to the BIA in trust for the Ho-Chunk Nation, with joint management of the entire 8,600-acre property by the tribe and state, which was to be worked out through a memorandum of understanding (MOU) and management plan. The formal link with the Ho-Chunk Nation was set, and after twenty years since the dam construction stoppage, progress was finally being made. However, there was a lot of work ahead to carry out the directives in WRDA.

4

Cliff Jumping

Reading the print version of the *Wisconsin State Journal* on Sunday mornings was a favorite weekly ritual at our home in Madison, and I was in the habit of glancing through the classified ads to see who was hiring. In May 1996, I came across a listing for a position with the newly created Kickapoo Reserve Management Board (KRMB) in La Farge. This ad caught my eye because we loved canoeing the Kickapoo River and camping in Wildcat Mountain State Park. My husband and I had camped there the previous September with a group of friends. The weather and fall colors were gorgeous, and we were some of the only campers in the park. In the morning, our tent flap opened to an incredible view of the Kickapoo Valley with a wispy line of fog tracing the outline of the river below as the cool fall air met the flowing water. It was one of those images I didn't need to photograph, as it will always be etched in my memory.

The classified ad also caught my eye because applications were due on June 6, 1996, the same date our first child was scheduled to be delivered. Being eight and a half months pregnant, I wasn't considering applying for anything other than an environmentally friendly diaper service.

In September of that year, I noticed the state of Wisconsin still hadn't filled that executive director position. Curiosity got the best of me, and I scheduled a meeting with State Senator Brian Rude, a person I had come to know and trust through my work on nonpoint source pollution rules and utility deregulation. I knew the Kickapoo River was in his district, and I hoped he'd know something about what was expected of the position.

He did.

Senator Rude did not gloss over the tumultuous history of the failed federal dam project and the frustration of the residents who had lived through it. He indicated that it would be a challenging job, given the negative impact to the community and the complexity of dealing with federal, state, and community stakeholders as well as the Ho-Chunk Nation. The initial request for applicants earlier in the year had not yielded a candidate the board was happy with, so they were trying again. "You should apply for it, but don't say I didn't warn you," he said with a slight smile.

The drive from Madison to La Farge for the interview on a gorgeous sun-drenched October afternoon sealed the deal. Heading northwest through the Wisconsin River Valley to Spring Green, where the sandhill cranes were starting to gather for their fall migration, and then driving through Richland Center to Viola, I finally reached the curves and hills of the Kickapoo Valley. I arrived a bit early and drove north of La Farge on State Highway 131 to Rockton, then pulled over at a spot where the rock outcroppings and Kickapoo River were separated only by the blacktop of County Highway P (now the Old 131 recreation trail). The river flowed gently and clearly, with the sun sparkling off the riffles where rocks and logs interrupted the southbound current. The fall colors were spectacular on the hillsides, and the nonexistent traffic led me to imagine not having to deal with the congestion and parking headaches of downtown Madison.

The Kickapoo Reserve Management Board members were warm, sincere, and charmingly informal during my interview. At one point, George Nettum, a KRMB board member I'd come to know through his county board role during my work with both the Wisconsin Land and Water Conservation Association and the Wisconsin Federation of Cooperatives, said, "I know you recently had a baby; who takes care of her? Do you plan to have another one anytime soon? Will you need a leave of absence?" I'm sure no human resources person would approve of those questions today, but in 1996, they seemed fitting for a group of citizens trying to make the best choice for their project. George's questions didn't come across as sexist because both the board and I knew full well how important it was to hire someone willing to commit themselves to the project at a very important stage of its development.

When I was offered the position, my husband and I discussed the issues surrounding my taking the job. We loved living in Madison with our new baby girl, and my husband had only one semester left to complete his master's degree in agronomy. But we also knew we wanted to try rural living, and this was a great opportunity. When I accepted the position, the weekly La Farge newspaper headline listed my salary in big bold letters, which I found amusing since I accepted a cut in pay from my previous position.

My official start date was to be December 16, 1996, but an important meeting was taking place in November between the Ho-Chunk Nation, the U.S. Army Corps of Engineers (COE) and the state of Wisconsin. I felt it would give me a better understanding of the project, so I went to the meeting at the Ho-Chunk Nation headquarters on my own time. The COE had requested the meeting to explain the federal legislation that would ultimately transfer 8,600 acres to the state of Wisconsin and the Ho-Chunk Nation to jointly manage as a public property. That's when I realized how naïve I was and how honest Brian Rude had been when he stated the job would be a challenge.

Hearing the Ho-Chunk Nation elders and legislators question the COE representatives and raise concerns about the intent of the state of Wisconsin during the meeting gave me a great deal to study prior to the official start of my new position. Politicians had lied to and cheated the Ho-Chunk ancestors; why would this promise of returning sacred land be any different? The Ho-Chunk legislators also indicated their previous president had negotiated this federal agreement without consulting the elders. He had settled for only 1,200 acres, while other tribal members believed the entire property should be returned to the Ho-Chunk people. Their frustration was palpable, and it was truly eye-opening to listen as an observer with no formal role to play at that point. It would be the first but not the last time I'd wonder what I'd gotten myself into.

What I had gotten myself into was a front-row seat in the

negotiations as the state of Wisconsin and the Ho-Chunk Nation began preparing for how to accept this amazing property and the responsibilities that came with it.

The people tasked with coming up with the required Memorandum of Understanding (MOU) included five representatives appointed by Governor Thompson to negotiate on behalf of the state of Wisconsin: Peter Helland, a friend of the governor, who had worked with Ho-Chunk Nation leaders on business projects; Dave Meier, who had served as a conservation warden in the Wisconsin Dells area and therefore knew some of the Ho-Chunk Nation leaders; Chris Spooner, the governor's staff advisor on environmental issues, who was to be the eyes and ears for Governor Thompson as the proceedings ensued; David Kluesner, formerly of the governor's staff and newly appointed to the KRMB; and board Chairman Ron Johnson, who had served as an advocate from the inception of the proposal. He provided the local perspective and motivation for getting the agreement done. The governor also directed the DNR to authorize attorney Mike Lutz to serve as the state's legal counsel. Mike had a wealth of experience in property negotiations and had worked through the contentious issue of tribal spear fishing in northern Wisconsin on behalf of the state in the 1980s. My role was to organize the meetings, take notes, and do whatever else it took to get the MOU done.

Although all the Ho-Chunk Nation legislators were listed as members of the team, five legislators were formally identified as the lead negotiators by their president, with confirmation by the tribal elders: Gerald Cleveland Sr., Kevin Greengrass, Robert Mudd, Clarence Pettibone, and Dallas Whitewing. Not only were they recognized as leaders through election by tribal members, but they were also students of their tribal history who understood the importance of the project and who would need to be involved from their independent, sovereign Nation to reach an agreement. Consultation with respected elders from each clan was also recognized early on as a requirement for the final agreement.

Over the course of a year, the negotiating team met repeatedly with the Ho-Chunk Nation elders and president, attorneys, and staff of every agency involved. The meetings were often tense. The tribal members were working through a variety of important issues following revisions to their constitution in 1994. With four branches of government dealing with housing, health care, preservation of traditional properties and language, gaming resources, and staffing issues, the leaders were spread thin, and the Kickapoo project was just one of many requiring their attention. The MOU was drafted and modified; meetings were scheduled and often rescheduled as the congressionally mandated deadline of October 31, 1997, loomed. (See further details about the negotiations in Chapter 6.)

I came out of one particularly tense meeting feeling especially depressed. An elder had spoken for at least twenty minutes about the treaty of 1837 that had resulted in the removal of their ancestors and told how the government had tricked their tribal representatives into signing it. His booming voice echoed off the meeting room walls as if he were an old-time gospel preacher. The art of using prolonged pauses, giving the listeners time to think, is incredibly effective, and he was skilled at this storytelling method. His words broke my heart. It was not what I had learned in history class or seen growing up. Their people had been tricked and removed from their lands, and my immigrant ancestors had played a part in causing this grief and hardship. It was amazing the tribal members were even willing to consider negotiating with us.

But a shared sense of protecting an ecological gem finally brought the various parties together, and the MOU was signed by Governor Thompson and Ho-Chunk Nation President Jacob Lonetree on October 30, 1997—one day before the deadline imposed by the 1996 Water Resources Development Act.

I had not yet been on the job a full year.

Shepherding a MOU to completion was just one aspect of my new job. Setting up a new office, hiring staff, exploring the property boundaries and features, learning the state system, meeting community leaders, and planning for the future of the project filled those early days. Al Anderson had returned to his regular position with UW-Extension, but we talked frequently. Sometimes he'd answer one of my questions with, "You and the board will need to figure that out." There was no instruction sheet or orientation manual for what needed to be done.

Other issues would slow the progress down during the next few years. Although the congressional directive in the WRDA was clear and $17 million had been authorized for the final transfer, this funding had not yet been included in any of the U.S. Army Corps of Engineers' annual budget requests to Congress, which kept the project at a standstill. We all learned quickly that funding authorization and appropriation are two very different things. In a nutshell, a federal agency has permission to request funds for projects if authorized, but to get funding requires an appropriation in their agency budget and approval by Congress.

Wisconsin's congressional delegation, including Senators Russ Feingold and Herb Kohl and—newly elected to the third district—Congressman Ron Kind and their incredibly dedicated staff, responded to annual requests from the KRMB and state officials to appropriate the money so the transfer could be completed. The Ho-Chunk Nation president and legislators would repeatedly submit letters of support and authorize members of their staff to testify at COE regional meetings, encouraging the Corps to fund the work and transfer the ownership of the land in a timely fashion. This pressure finally paid off when a quitclaim deed transferring the land from the COE to the state of Wisconsin was prepared.

Real estate specialists for the COE, state of Wisconsin, and Ho-Chunk Nation checked and rechecked the description of boundaries for the roughly 7,400 acres to be transferred to the state and 1,200 acres to the BIA in trust for the Ho-Chunk Nation. As a courtesy, they would send me each draft via fax, but the language of quarter-quarter section lines in the land survey descriptions was foreign to me. I verified the overall township names and total acreages and hoped for the best. The often-referred-to 9,000 acres had included some easements that were no longer needed, so the document verified that 8,600 acres was more accurate and would become the new referenced size of the Reserve.

I left for Madison before sunrise on December 28, 2000, knowing I wouldn't get home until after dark, given the shortened daylight hours of Wisconsin winter. It was important the quitclaim deed get registered with the Vernon County Register of Deeds at the courthouse in Viroqua before the end of the year, and I still needed the secretary of the Department of Administration and his attorney to do the final review and sign the paperwork. Not only did the quitclaim deed make the transfer of ownership official, but if I could get it registered prior to the end of the calendar year, local units of government would receive payments in lieu of taxes for the year 2000. The Wisconsin Department of Revenue had estimated the value of the roughly 7,200 acres of state-owned land at $3,075,100, which was then used to calculate payments to Vernon County, Western Wisconsin Technical College, local schools, and the towns of Stark, Whitestown, and Forest where the property is located. Loss of property tax revenue since 1975 was frustrating for the local governments and school districts impacted by the project. Annual reliable payments based on the equalized land value for a property requiring few public services would help smooth relations within the region.

Due to the holidays, the Department of Administration (DOA) building was nearly empty when I got there. A directory in the lobby indicated the secretary of the DOA's office was on the top floor. Stepping off the elevator, I'm sure I let out an audible *wow*. Even in December, the lake view reminded me why our Wisconsin forefathers chose Madison as the capital city.

Despite all the phone calls and emails about the preparations for the closing documents, the receptionist still had to spend time tracking down the attorney I had been working with for more than a year. The Wisconsin DOA officials had had the MOU since it was signed in October, and the real estate description had been faxed the week prior to my visit. When I first discussed it with the attorney via phone, he had asked more than once how much the state was paying for the land. "Nothing—no cost to the state for the land; it's a government-to-government transfer," I'd say, and his response was always, "Really? Are you sure?"

The receptionist finally found the attorney, and we went through the document one more time in person. While we were waiting for the secretary's signature, the attorney mentioned he'd never been to the Kickapoo Valley but that he'd like to visit someday. Comments like that made me appreciate the citizens who prioritized the need for local management of the property through the KRMB so that those making the decisions had some ties to the land, rather than disconnected government employees.

The DOA secretary at the time, George Lightbourn, was formal but friendly, and I relaxed a bit when I realized he understood the deadline pressure I was under. He offered a bit of a warning about "getting what you wish for," but he signed the quitclaim deed accepting the land on behalf of the state, and I was finally able to head to Viroqua, hoping I would get there before the courthouse closed at four o'clock. I couldn't help thinking about what would happen if I had an accident. Would anyone pick up the envelope and get it to the courthouse in time? Would the communities get their payments? Most importantly, I knew the document ensured the land could finally be permanently protected with no threat of damming the Kickapoo River.

Thankfully, the return trip was without incident, and the quitclaim deed for the 7,400 acres that were being transferred from the COE to the state of Wisconsin was submitted by hand to the Vernon County Register of Deeds office on December 28, 2000, with an hour to spare. Had cell phones been common at the time, the selfie would have been my profile picture for years. Instead, the registrar's stamp and a clean copy for the KVR file cabinet was documentation enough.

Five months later, the COE provided documentation to the BIA that transferred 1,200 acres to be held in trust for the Ho-Chunk Nation. Trust status has a sordid history for tribes throughout the country. In brief, it evolved after the General Allotment Act of 1887 failed to protect lands staying in Indian ownership. The act basically set up a system where, after a twenty-five-year allotment to a tribal member expired, the land was often transferred to white settlers. Even if multimember acreage became too complex to confirm tribal members' formal ownership, the land would be made available to settlers. Once again, tribal members were taken advantage of on everything from mineral rights to productive agricultural lands, as the system of land ownership reflected the U.S. government's model, not the tribe's.

The Indian Reorganization Act of 1934 ended the allotment process and ensured that lands held in trust were protected for the recognized tribe indefinitely. The federal government, through the Department of the Interior's Bureau of Indian Affairs, holds nearly all tribal lands in trust with an intended layer of protections for their interests. It's not my place to indicate whether the process is best for all Indian Country, but during my tenure at the KVR, I would come to witness the benefits for the Ho-Chunk Nation to request assistance through the BIA on land management, equipment, research, and funding for significant projects under the trust status.

The formalization of trust status documents was completed at the official dedication ceremony, and a celebration was held on May 11, 2001, at what would become the site of the Kickapoo Valley Reserve Visitor Center. In attendance were Ho-Chunk Nation dancers, tribal members, elders, and elected officials; students from the La Farge and Ontario schools; former landowners displaced by the dam and lake project; senators and representatives past and present; and staff members from various federal, state, and local agencies. The Ho-Chunk Nation dancers and drum circle performed, followed by an elder providing a prayer and explaining the tradition of burying tobacco in honor of the ancestors and in blessing for the future of the land. Despite the chilly gray spring day, the mood was celebratory, and every speaker noted how the land had come full circle. Both Native and white ancestors had been removed from the land, and now it was returning to all the people as public property, forever protected by an improbable coalition of advocates with a formal commitment to the Kickapoo River Valley.

5
Backpaddle

In order to better understand the remarkable and unprecedented government action that turned a failed federal project to structurally control a free-flowing river into what would become a publicly owned nature reserve, I need to backpaddle a bit for perspective on what was happening beyond the Kickapoo River Valley at a national level, and how those events affected and helped shape the actions and policy decisions of local and state leaders involved in the Kickapoo River's fate.

Although concerns about the human impact on the environment had existed in North America for hundreds of years, the widespread popularity of books like Rachel Carson's 1962 *Silent Spring* and Edward Abbey's 1968 *Desert Solitaire* became a call to action in a country recovering from the stress of the Vietnam War. With a television in nearly every house, Americans could see the environmental and human health impacts of Agent Orange and DDT and watch Ohio's Cuyahoga River burn and Wisconsin's Fox River burp methane gas bubbles. An organized and active environmental movement began to take shape in the early 1960s, with the civil rights and antiwar demonstrations providing a precedent for activism and making news.

The movement reached a crescendo when Wisconsin Senator Gaylord Nelson instituted the first Earth Day in the spring of 1970.

While it was initially created as a teach-in, twenty million Americans took to the streets, parks, and auditoriums to demonstrate for a healthy and sustainable environment in massive coast-to-coast rallies on April 22, 1970, and thousands of colleges and universities organized protests on environmental issues. Groups that had been fighting against oil and sewage spills, industrial pollution, toxic dumps, damage from pesticides, the building of freeways, the loss of wilderness, and the extinction of wildlife realized they shared common values and could enact real change for the better through coordinated efforts at the federal level.

The passage of the National Environmental Policy Act of 1969, the Clean Air Act of 1970, and the Clean Water Act of 1972 directed the federal agencies how to do better in protecting the environment.

The Effect of the National Environmental Policy Act on the Kickapoo Valley

The National Environmental Policy Act (NEPA) was enacted to "promote efforts which will prevent or eliminate damage to the environment and biosphere and stimulate the health and welfare of man; to enrich the understanding of the ecological systems and natural resources important to the Nation; and to establish a Council on Environmental Quality."[4]

NEPA required that an environmental impact statement (EIS) be drafted for all federal projects, which meant that agency employees and federal decision-makers had to have all the information about possible impacts on the environment prior to proceeding with a project and had to have considered alternatives that reduced those impacts. Equally important was the requirement for public input during the EIS process and the authority given to the Council on Environmental Quality and to the Environmental Protection Agency to review federal agency statements. Individuals and organizations now had access to information about federal projects and could comment directly on the findings, as public hearings and testimony were embedded in the process.

The legislation required that the environmental impact statement address the following:

4 National Environmental Policy Act, 1969, Sec 2 (42 U.S. Code 4321), https://www.fsa.usda.gov/Internet/FSA_File/nepa_statute.pdf.

> (i) the environmental impact of the proposed action, (ii) any adverse environmental effects which cannot be avoided should the proposal be implemented, (iii) alternatives to the proposed action, (iv) the relationship between local short-term uses of man's environment and the maintenance and enhancement of long-term productivity, and (v) any irreversible and irretrievable commitments of resources which would be involved in the proposed action should it be implemented.[5]

By the time the nation's legislative process was catching up to the environmental movement, the La Farge Lake and Dam project was already mired in debate and bureaucracy.

Reflecting the newness of the NEPA requirements, the draft EIS prepared by the Corps of Engineers in November 1970 for the La Farge Lake and Dam project was a mere ten pages long. Although assumed to be written with good intent, the discussion of environmental considerations was cursory at best, and the agency succinctly concluded that the potential benefits to the communities, in terms of flood control and economic development around the proposed lake, outweighed the impact on natural resources in the project area.

The draft EIS triggered public input from near and far. Groups like the Sierra Club and the Citizens Natural Resources Association utilized the previous inventories of botanists, birders, and archaeologists to challenge the COE methods and findings on the project. Opposition to such projects was becoming a nationwide trend. On February 20, 1972, the *New York Times* reported that "fifteen of the embattled corps's major undertakings—worth a total of several billion dollars in planned expenditures—are now bogged down in lawsuits and controversy, some before the bulldozers could start, others in mid-ditch."[6] Well beyond mid-ditch, land for this project had been purchased and the construction of the dam and water control tower was well underway.

The Introduction of the *Final Environmental Statement, La Farge Lake, Kickapoo River*, gives evidence of the influence politics played, where

---

5 National Environmental Policy Act of 1969 Sec. 102 [42 USC $ 4332], NEPA1969Sec102.

6 John Noble Wilford, "Corps of Engineers Caught Up in Battle of the Builders Against the Preservers," New York Times, Feb. 20, 1972, https://www.nytimes.com/1972/02/20/archives/corps-of-engineers-caught-up-in-battle-of-the-builders-against-the.html.

concerns expressed by Governor Lucey (previously a supporter of the project) are referenced as justification for revisions to the federal process:

> Governor Patrick J. Lucey of Wisconsin and General Ernest Graves, Division Engineer, North Central Division, U.S. Army Corps of Engineers have expressed mutual concern that adverse effects upon the environment due to construction of the proposed La Farge Lake must be minimized. Certain tasks necessary to meet this objective were not contemplated at the time the initial environmental impact statement was prepared and submitted to the Council on Environmental Quality in January 1971.[7]

The request for the revised EIS required additional study of the following:

- The existing values of the Kickapoo River
- A broader range of alternatives, including a dry reservoir or smaller dam
- The project's impact on stream fishery above and below the dam
- The effects upon wildlife and wildlife habitat

Timing was of the essence in the project's EIS process. The eighty-two-page revised EIS was distributed in September 1971 to federal and state agencies and organizations that had commented on the original, and they were asked in the transmittal letter to respond within thirty days. Agencies and organizations commenting on the revised EIS expressed frustration with the short time frame, and environmental groups interpreted the short turnaround as a foregone conclusion that the findings in the EIS would make little to no difference in the project's outcome. They noted that the COE was ready to award the contract work for the dam outflow system in the spring of 1972.

In a letter to the attorneys representing the environmental groups, General Rodney Cox of the COE referenced the "learning process"

---

7 *Final Environmental Statement: La Farge Lake, Kickapoo River, Vernon County, Wisconsin*, U.S. Army Engineer District, St. Paul, MN, February 18, 1972, https://search.worldcat.org/title/27307563.

in preparing environmental statements that he felt was due to the newness of the NEPA requirements. He also stated that "traditionally in the United States, development of the Nation's resources has been left to the professionals." He then tried to assure readers that "our environmental impact statement is directed toward all professional planners and interested parties in public life; we in the Corps are still faced with the rather traditional disagreements between upstream and downstream interest; the public interest is changing with increasing interest in environmental quality and resource scarcity." Noteworthy too is the dilemma that General Cox describes as the COE's being "caught in a conflicting situation where Congress has told us to follow the guidelines in NEPA but has authorized and funded projects to construct."

Eric Epstein was a young activist who would later become involved in the Kickapoo Valley Reserve project as an employee of the Wisconsin DNR, and he is arguably one of the best ecologists Wisconsin has ever known. When I met with him to discuss the demise of the lake and dam project specifically, he elaborated on the importance of the federal policies' impact on environmental issues of the early 1970s, saying, "The EIS process at least forced the Corps of Engineers to ask and answer questions." No doubt that exercise intensified the public understanding and scrutiny of the proposed dam and lake.

In the concluding statement, General Cox summed up the revised environmental impact statement:

> The final EIS for the La Farge Lake project concludes with significant references to mitigating adverse effects when possible, arguing further that the adverse effects have been considered, yet the action is fully consistent with national policy laws and administrative directives; it concludes that the total public interest is best served by its implementation.[8]

Despite General Cox's assurances, the question of whether the public would be best served by damming the Kickapoo River at La Farge still remained in many people's minds. Elected officials,

---

8 *Final Environmental Statement: La Farge Lake, Kickapoo River, Vernon County, Wisconsin*, U.S. Army Engineer District, St. Paul, MN, February 18, 1972, https://search.worldcat.org/title/27307563.

environmental groups, and residents were caught up in an argument between ballooning construction costs, scientific evaluations, and environmental protection on the one hand, and economic development and flood control on the other, and the conclusion in the final EIS would be challenged for years to come.

The Clean Water Act Plays a Role Too

The Federal Water Pollution Control Act of 1948 was amended in 1972 and became known as the Clean Water Act (CWA), which had important implications for the development of the Kickapoo Valley Reserve because it recognized the need to prevent pollution and protect water quality. Significant new components were added to the original 1948 act, and the revised legislation focused on restoring and maintaining the chemical, physical, and biological integrity of the nation's waters through three ambitious goals:

1. Discharge of pollutants into navigable waters be eliminated by 1985.
2. Wherever attainable, an interim goal of water quality that protects and propagates fish and wildlife and allows recreation in and on the water must be achieved by July 1, 1983.
3. Discharge of toxic pollutants in toxic amounts be prohibited.

Federal and state roles were also addressed in the legislation. Most water quality standards are set at the federal level, and states are responsible for the implementation and enforcement authority to meet those standards. Thanks in large part to the environmental movement, the House and Senate passed the CWA by an overwhelming majority, but President Richard Nixon vetoed the act because he felt that the "extreme and needless" spending in the legislation would not serve the public interest. Democrats held the majority in both the House and Senate in 1972, and the CWA had received bipartisan support, so the Republican president's veto was overridden by well more than the two-thirds vote required by the Constitution.

The second goal of the CWA, to protect waterways for aquatic life and recreation, was especially significant in the context of the La Farge Lake and Dam project, and Wisconsin was well-equipped to implement the new water quality standards because of the strong conservation ethic in both the University of Wisconsin system and the DNR.

Important in the political arena were Wisconsin Senator Gaylord Nelson, a well-known environmental advocate, and Senator William Proxmire, a budget hawk and the creator of the Golden Fleece Award that focused attention on wasteful federal projects. Senator Nelson repeatedly expressed concerns about the water quality of the proposed lake, and Senator Proxmire questioned the rapidly increasing costs incurred during initial construction. Wisconsin's governors during this period were also environmental advocates. Republican Warren Knowles (1965–1971) is in the Wisconsin Conservation Hall of Fame in recognition of his work protecting wetlands and water quality. Democrat Patrick Lucey (1971–1977) was an advocate for outdoor recreation and worked to enhance the state park system. He was also a native of southwest Wisconsin with ties to Ferryville and De Soto near the Mississippi River.

Correspondence between constituents, agencies, environmental advocates, and these elected leaders repeatedly stressed the importance of letting the NEPA process and CWA standards determine the fate of the La Farge Lake and Dam project. Noteworthy is the obvious disdain Senator Nelson had for the Corps of Engineers and their work throughout the nation. The COE apparently had a reputation for wielding power over legislators by selectively prioritizing their projects in politicians' districts. Senator Nelson responded on November 22, 1972, to a resident of Ontario, Wisconsin, regarding his vote to withhold funds for the La Farge project until a comprehensive EIS was completed:

> Fighting the Corps of Engineers is a tough business, as I have found out after years of doing battle with them. They have the political power in the Congress to win almost every cause they support. There are some hopeful signs that the Congress is prepared to place Corps projects under more careful scrutiny. Let's hope so, or else within a few years our last free-flowing river will be just a memory.

Academia Weighs In

I can only imagine the level of frustration for those arguing against the dam and those who supported it, not to mention the COE supervisors under pressure from members of Congress and environmental activists. Contracting with the University of Wisconsin-Madison to further study the potential impacts of the dam and lake may have eased the pressure for a time.

Initially proposed as a three-year project, the final time frame was fifteen months in order to include two growing seasons. Experts from the Nelson Institute for Environmental Studies (IES) at UW-Madison were charged with providing a report covering four main categories of impact: nutrients, socioeconomic aspects, hydrology and sedimentation and biological impacts (wildlife, invertebrate fauna, downstream cold-water fishery, terrestrial vegetation, and aquatic vegetation).

The report, entitled "Environmental Analysis of the Kickapoo River Impoundment: A Report to the U.S. Army Corps of Engineers," was completed in November 1974. Each category includes what research and studies were done and the corresponding conclusions and recommendations. The potential for significant impact was clear in each category, as were options to minimize the impacts and cost estimates to do so. I met with Professor Dennis Keeney to discuss the report and his work as one of the principal investigators on the study. Although the report is more than 300 typewritten pages, Dr. Keeney shared that the placement of the conclusion for nitrogen and phosphorus on page one was the proverbial nail in the coffin from his perspective:

> The La Farge impoundment will produce a lake of relatively poor water quality as compared to lakes in northern Wisconsin due to the fact that the Kickapoo River has a high concentration of dissolved nitrogen and phosphorus.[9]

Recommendations included efforts to minimize algal blooms by upgrading sewage treatment plants, instituting erosion control practices on agricultural fields, and preventing animal waste discharge from farms in the upper watershed. Cost estimates were in the millions of dollars for initial improvements that would require ongoing commitments by communities and landowners and ongoing expenditures to implement the practices if the lake were to

9 "Environmental Analysis of the Kickapoo River Impoundment: A Report to the U.S. Army Corps of Engineers," UW Madison Institute for Environmental Studies, November 1974.

be suitable for recreation.

The IES report addressed the issues, as directed by NEPA and CWA, and the congressional leaders referenced it to halt the funding for the project, which in turn ended construction activity by the Corps in 1975.

Empowering Native Americans

President Nixon is usually not the first politician who comes to mind when we think about protecting the environment, but his tenure includes some of the most important environmental laws ever written. This might not have been his first choice of legislation, but public sentiment and timing encouraged the Republican president to collaborate with the Democrats in Congress, and as previously mentioned, bipartisanship is one of the common threads that runs through the story of the Kickapoo Valley Reserve.

In addition to the National Environmental Policy Act, Richard Nixon is credited with enacting laws that transformed federal policy concerning Native Americans. It's hard for me to imagine now, but in 1953, the federal government adopted a policy that was described as an attempt to assimilate Native Americans into the United States and subject them to the same laws as other citizens. The Indian Termination Policy of 1953 stripped Native American tribes of their rights to sacred lands, federal assistance, and public education. During his presidency, Nixon collaborated with congressional Democrats and signed fifty-two measures in support of tribal sovereignty. Before resigning in 1974, he initiated what has come to be known in Indian Country as his greatest contribution: The Indian Self-Determination and Education Assistance Act, which officially reversed the 1953 policy and authorized government agencies to work directly with tribes, and for tribes to administer federal programs to their members.

These expansive laws all played an important role in making the Kickapoo Valley Reserve a reality. They enabled Congress to deauthorize the La Farge Lake and Dam project in the Water Resources Development Act of 1996 and approve the land transfer to the state of Wisconsin and the Ho-Chunk Nation. Throughout the negotiations for the transfer, the Corps of Engineers staff took great pains to include their colleagues in the Bureau of Indian Affairs, the Advisory Council on Historic Preservation, the Wisconsin State Historic Preservation Office, and the Ho-Chunk Nation's Department of Heritage Preservation, Cultural Resource Division, through meeting invitations and encouraging comments on draft documents. I believe the Memorandum of Understanding, Joint Management Plan, and Programmatic Agreement have stood the test of time due to the collaborative nature from which they developed.

6
The Confluence

The Water Resources Development Act (WRDA) is a lengthy biennial piece of federal legislation that is the primary mechanism for authorizing water projects to be studied, planned, and developed by the U.S. Army Corps of Engineers (COE) throughout the United States and its territories. The role the WRDA played as the confluence that brought a resolution to the boondoggle of the La Farge Lake and dam is so unique that it merits additional explanation in this chapter.

After a variety of reviews, cost-benefit analyses, and glimmers of hope that the 70 percent completed La Farge Lake and Dam project would eventually be finished, the 1996 WRDA ended a dispute that had been ongoing since 1975. The act deauthorized the project and laid out a road map for the land's future. Wisconsin Senator Russ Feingold and 3rd District Congressman Steve Gunderson took the lead on drafting the language directing the land transfer from the COE to the BIA and the state of Wisconsin. The action was endorsed and protected from procedural hurdles by other leaders in the bipartisan Wisconsin legislative delegation, including Senator Herb Kohl and Congressmen Tom Petri and David Obey.

Congressman Gunderson used a visual breakdown of the cost savings to convince his colleagues in June 1994 why it would be considerably cheaper to shut down the project and transfer the land than to complete the dam and lake. Comparing the proposed transfer cost of $17 million to the amount already spent on construction, the losses to the local economy, and an estimate of funds needed to complete the project, Gunderson illustrated that a savings of $66 million would be achieved if the project was deauthorized and the land transferred.

From the Congressional Record, June 14, 1994:

> $5.5 million authorized, La Farge lake and dam, 1962
>
> $18 million actually spent by the COE on the project
>
> $8 million estimated in losses for the local economy, 1990
>
> $102 million if the project were to be completed in 1994 dollars
>
> $17 million authorized to be appropriated for the completion of cleanup and highway relocation
>
> Transfer to state and Ho-Chunk Nation results in savings to federal taxpayers: $66 million [over $130 million in 2024][10]

This justification helped garner support for Section 361 of the WRDA and set conditions for the Corps of Engineers to do the following:

- Clean up the land and verify boundaries.
- Fund highway reconstruction.
- Put to rest any efforts to complete the dam through deauthorization of the project.
- Set parameters for the state of Wisconsin and Ho-Chunk Nation to write and agree to a memorandum of understanding.
- Ensure the protection of environmental, cultural, and archeological features.

The COE was being forced to disentangle itself from a thirty-year-old conundrum, and everyone involved wanted to make sure it got done right.

---

10 Congressman Steve Gundersen presentation during floor session in the House of Representatives, June 14, 1994. Narrative found on pages 12875–12876 Congressional Record, https://www.congress.gov/bound-congressional-record/1994/06/14/house-section

As part of the transfer requirements, the COE justifiably insisted on a hold harmless agreement (HHA) to indemnify the federal government from being held liable by the state of Wisconsin. For twenty years, the COE had been embroiled in various lawsuits filed by environmental groups over the La Farge Lake and Dam project and had been dealing with former landowners who were demanding either their land back or more compensation since the reason for invoking eminent domain was no longer valid. The HHA was a concession to the COE's desire to put an end to this legal wrangling, but it would prove to be a bureaucratic nightmare for the state of Wisconsin's attorneys. Given the history of the property and the lack of on-site management through the years, no one could predict future problems or whether former landowners would continue to challenge the ownership of the land. Mike Lutz, a member of the team negotiating the MOU, worked with the Department of Administration's attorneys and other appointed officials to draft the HHA.

Identifying hazardous sites in need of cleanup revealed a range of problems, from lead pollution in a field long used for trapshooting to soil contaminated with oil and gasoline at the site of a former automotive garage. The WRDA language directed that the worst sites be dealt with by the COE prior to the ownership transfer. Nonetheless, the state of Wisconsin's attorneys were concerned that something might have been overlooked that would require potentially expensive remedies in the future.

Meetings were held, and discussions ensued. Eventually, elected officials convinced the attorneys that the state of Wisconsin was willing to inherit the property, potential problems and all. A clause was included in the final quitclaim deed, saying that the state of Wisconsin would consider "the United States free from all claims and damages arising from or through the ownership, operation, and/or maintenance of the land and improvements on the property to be conveyed." According to Mike Lutz, the wording "to the extent allowed by law" in the final language of the HHA protected the state, as the Wisconsin Constitution does not allow a promise of future debt. If a problem did arise, it would be dealt with like any other problem on property owned by the state.

Fortunately, there have been no lawsuits in the two decades that have elapsed. The directives in the WRDA, the trust status with the

BIA, the registration of the deed proving ownership by the state, the diligence of the cleanup efforts, the clarification of state authority through Wisconsin Statute 41.41, and the agreement with the Ho-Chunk Nation have thus far prevented the problems the state's attorneys feared.

Unchartered Waters via an MOU

The WRDA's directive requiring that a Memorandum of Understanding between the state of Wisconsin and the Ho-Chunk Nation be drafted was another hurdle to be cleared. There were no examples anywhere in the United States of a sovereign nation and a state government sharing the ownership and management responsibilities of a publicly held property—and to my knowledge, the KVR is still the only model of this kind of cooperation.

How this unusual marriage came about is a story in itself. Following the failure of the 1994 Water Resources Development Act in the Senate, leaders from the Ho-Chunk Nation were made aware of the issues surrounding the property by Al Anderson and his work with the local advisory committee. Tribal Chair JoAnn Jones sent a letter to the BIA expressing interest in taking over all COE-owned acres through the federal procedure for getting rid of "surplus property." A surplus property is usually declared when a project exists for ten years or more without federal expenditures. But the COE had not declared the La Farge property as surplus due to the appropriations in their 1986 through 1988 federal fiscal years, the continued studies of alternatives over the years, and the proposal from Congressmen Gunderson and Petri for the entire property to transfer to the state in the 1994 WRDA draft.

So the stage was set for the state and Ho-Chunk Nation to work together if the project was to move forward. Stories relayed to me vary on how it evolved from a request for the entire property to the final language transferring 1,200 acres to a trust administered by the BIA. One version I heard had the Ho-Chunk Nation President Chloris Lowe Jr. tucking his long black braid into his coat and covertly visiting with residents in the Kickapoo Valley at a local restaurant and hearing stories of the devastating personal and community impacts the project had caused. This convinced him the tribe's taking over the whole property would be a public relations nightmare and not worth pursuing.

The more political version of the story links a congressional proposal in the 1995 federal budget to impose an additional tax on tribal casino gaming to the outcome of the Kickapoo Valley project. The Ho-Chunk Nation opposed the higher tax because they operated one of the largest casinos in Wisconsin. Notes in the history files imply that the Wisconsin delegation would oppose the tax option if the Ho-Chunk Nation agreed to less acreage in the Kickapoo Valley. Whether it was a trip to the valley or political hardball, the outcome is 1,200 acres being held in trust by the BIA for the Ho-Chunk Nation and joint management of the entire property with the state of Wisconsin through the KRMB.

After meeting with Senator Feingold, Congressman Gunderson, and State Senator Brian Rude, President Lowe provided an agreement in principle on November 7, 1995. The principles included:

- Recognition of "culturally significant sites" that supported the Ho-Chunk Nation's interest in the Kickapoo Valley.
- Protection of the most significant sites by a transfer to the BIA for the Ho-Chunk Nation that would not exceed 1,200 acres.
- Assurance the archeological sites would not be marked or fenced by any party.
- A process would be developed to protect sites that might not yet have been documented or inventoried at the time.
- The addition of two voting members nominated by the Ho-Chunk president and legislature to the Kickapoo Reserve Management Board.
- The land would be managed to preserve its natural condition and preclude commercial development.

Negotiations to turn these principles into an MOU and a joint management plan were frustratingly difficult from my vantage point due to the lack of trust prevalent on all sides. Local representatives didn't trust the COE because of the failed dam project, Ho-Chunk Nation leaders didn't trust the federal government due to the history of broken treaties, and the representatives of the COE didn't trust that Congress would actually fund everything required for the transfer.

The October 31, 1997, deadline imposed by the 1996 WRDA was both a blessing and a curse. This looming deadline was the catalyst needed to force the group to meet. Governor Tommy Thompson and the Ho-Chunk Nation legislature each appointed five members to the negotiating team, which included Ho-Chunk Nation legislators, KRMB members, and representatives from the governor's staff. The negotiators had a slew of support staff, which evolved into an ad hoc committee that would report to the negotiating team. The ad hoc committee included attorneys for both parties, archeology experts from the Corps, Ho-Chunk Nation and State Historical Society staff, UW–Madison representatives, and me—the recently hired executive director for the KRMB. The negotiating team met monthly, and the ad hoc group met biweekly in addition to attending the negotiating team meetings. Although some things could be addressed through email or fax, most of the meetings were in person, which added travel to Black River Falls or La Farge as part of the coordination. The Ho-Chunk Nation eventually moved a modified trailer to the site for their staff to use as an office to work from with a landline phone and dial-up computer connection.

Initial meetings focused on providing background information. Understanding where the property was, why it had such an unusual boundary and difficult history, and interpreting the brief WRDA language took up most of the meeting time. Tribal elders schooled the state representatives on the history of their people, the previous wrongs committed through treaties, and the lack of trust the broken promises continued to cause. All the while, the divisions within the Ho-Chunk Nation clans became more apparent. Some tribal leaders indicated that the previous president, Chloris Lowe Jr., had not consulted with the legislators and elders prior to agreeing to the 1,200 acres. At one particularly tense meeting on April 11, 1997, the highly respected elders Willard Lonetree and Orville Greendeer indicated that the tribe must have been an "afterthought" in the WRDA legislation. Their new understanding of the significance of this property to their ancestors made them question whether the tribe should delay the transfer and have authority over the entire 8,600 acres.

The KRMB representatives passionately repeated the federal and state legislative commitments to protect the entire property, as outlined in the WRDA and the Citizen Advisory Committee proposal. Mr. Lonetree calmly replied, "Okay, these statements brought the response I was looking for, and we will continue the dialogue," according to my shaky handwritten notes from the meeting.

A high priority was to inventory areas on the property that had not been checked for archeological sites in the surveys done in the 1960s and early 1970s when the dam and lake planning was in full swing. In the winter months of 1996–97, Ho-Chunk Nation staff and a team of students from UW–Madison evaluated previous studies and prepared maps of areas that still needed to be inventoried to get ready for ground-truthing the property and its archeological sites in the spring.

As Ho-Chunk Nation staff videotaped areas within the property for viewing by the elders, I recall thinking how ingenious it was to use this technology as part of the orientation. Recognized as relics today compared to cell phone capabilities, the hand-held video cameras used by the staff were roughly the size of a football and produced fairly clear pictures. At that time, few members of the tribal leadership had been to the property, as their headquarters were more than an hour away in Black River Falls. If a picture is worth a thousand words, a video was an even better way to show the beauty of the Kickapoo River and Valley and its rock outcroppings, some of which included petroglyphs, ceremonial sites, marker trees, and the scenic landscape in need of protection.

Ground-penetrating radar was utilized to determine burial sites, but the technology was relatively new, and there was a great deal of discussion between the archaeologists and Ho-Chunk Nation members about how accurate it was. After multiple discussions in meetings about the importance of keeping the locations of significant sites confidential, I found it ironic that the vegetation at suspected sites had to be mowed for the radar to work. In the Weister Creek quadrant, there were a series of bald spots for all to see during the spring inventory. Fortunately, the vegetation grew back, but this illustrated how technology and cultural protection can occasionally clash.

The Nation's staff also drew one-acre circles around each significant site to help identify which 1,200 acres should be held in trust. It soon became clear that 1,200 one-acre sites would be a nightmare to survey, describe in land records, and manage for public access. Instead, the visual map of the significant archeological sites showed two areas of concentrated historic use.

The Ho-Chunk Nation opted for two large blocks of land that

included the highest concentrations of significant sites (370 acres in the Black Hawk Rock quadrant and 830 acres in the northern quadrant). In addition, wording was added to both the programmatic agreement and the MOU that required the state to pass legislation protecting sites on the state's land at the same level as federal ownership would. Desecration of an archeological site at the federal level can include jail time, significant fines, and the confiscation of private property used to commit the crime.

Despite this headway, negotiations stalled in May 1997 as the Ho-Chunk Nation held elections, resulting in a new president and three new legislators joining the negotiating team. It was about that same time when Rex Whitegull, a soft-spoken tribal member who got to know the land while helping document medicinal plants and ceremonial sites, told me, "Your greatest lesson in this process of dealing with the tribe will be patience."

The interagency ad hoc group and support staff continued working on the programmatic agreement language specific to protecting cultural and archeological sites, and the joint management plan was starting to take shape. The joint management plan is not a technical document by any means but more of a laundry list of what each side could and couldn't live with when managing the property. Tribal officials were sworn in in July, which meant schedules didn't allow the negotiating team to meet until August, and a bit of catch-up was needed for some of the newly elected Ho-Chunk Nation leaders. With the October deadline quickly approaching, the pressure was on for the completion of documents and maps.

Legal instruments, such as covenants and easements for the protection of significant sites, were considered and dismissed as there were so many throughout the project area. It was decided that using the state's rule-making process and authority for on-site enforcement was the best alternative—but this required the Ho-Chunk Nation and the archaeologists to trust the state and especially the KRMB. A clause establishing a way to mediate disputes was included, just in case mutual trust didn't stand the test of time.

The roller coaster of negotiating continued with the Ho-Chunk Nation's contract attorney repeatedly recommending to the ad hoc group that the two sides should request an extension to the October 30 deadline from the Corps. Staff for both sides rejected this recommendation out of a shared fear the momentum would be lost, even though the group was struggling with what needed to be in the MOU.

One September evening, I was reviewing meeting notes while watching *Late Night with David Letterman*, and I came up with a non-comedic "Top Ten" list that would become the working draft of the MOU. The ten statements nearly wrote themselves once I concentrated only on protecting cultural sites and the environmentally significant aspects of the property:

1. The Reserve will be preserved in a natural state and developed only to the extent necessary to enhance outdoor recreational and educational opportunities.
2. The Reserve will be managed as one continuous parcel of land or reserve following the policies in the management plan and administered through the KRMB.
3. The lands to be transferred in trust for the Nation are those portions of Sections 4, 22, and 23 up to 1,200 acres designated by the Ho-Chunk Nation.
4. The management plan will be reviewed by the state and Nation annually for the first five years and every five years thereafter.
5. The board agrees to limit public disclosure of the location of each archeological site.
6. The state will add two voting representatives of the Nation to the board.
7. The board and Nation will develop a memorandum of agreement within one year to address enforcement of the Reserve's policies and procedures to enforce laws on the Reserve.
8. In balance with the state responsibility, the Nation may pay a sum sufficient in lieu of taxes to the local governmental units affected by trust lands.
9. The management plan will include a method to transfer to the Ho-Chunk Nation any additional significant archeological sites discovered.
10. The state and Nation jointly request that the simultaneous transfer of the entire 8,600 acres from the U.S. Army Corps of Engineers to the state and the Bureau of Indian

> Affairs in trust for the Nation as required by the Water Resources Development Act of 1996 be no later than January 1, 1999.

The full negotiating team met on September 15 in the Ho-Chunk Nation conference room attached to the casino in Baraboo. My top ten list had been distributed to all parties via email with the hope it would break the stalemate by giving everyone something to look at. Rumors suggesting the negotiations were failing had reached the team members, and a letter had been sent to Governor Thompson from Chuck Kingswan of the Ho-Chunk Nation, expressing frustration with these insinuations. At one point during the meeting, the attorneys and support staff were asked to leave the room. Following this closed-door meeting, the state and tribal representatives publicly committed to meeting the October deadline. In addition, Willard Lonetree made a pointed comment about his impression that there may be some in attendance who were more interested in billable hours than in working toward a solution, and he encouraged those people to leave. Many eyes looked at the floor or ceiling to avoid eye contact, but nobody left.

Progress continued as I tried to edit the draft based on comments heard at the meetings. Members of the negotiating team and supporting staff had repeatedly brought up possible issues that might surface when dealing with public property of such a significant size. What types of recreation would be allowed? How do we protect undocumented archeological sites? Who will enforce archeological and environmental protection? Drafts and redrafts were shared via fax and emails through the ad hoc group right up to the deadline. Software editing didn't exist, so the various agency and tribal recipients would print the draft, mark it up, and fax it back to the whole group with proposed changes. I'd wait for a call or email from every member agreeing to the change, then change the original. Attorneys inserted formal legal language, spelled out a few things more clearly, and added an eleventh clause, but essentially, the top ten list had survived the revision process.

Once the documents were finalized, I assumed that planning the signing ceremony would be an easier and much more enjoyable task.

Wrong. Given the short notice and numerous commitments already on Governor Thompson's and newly elected Ho-Chunk Nation President Lonetree's calendars, the scheduling was a challenge in itself.

Thursday, October 30—one day before the federal deadline—was the only option for hosting this historic event on the property. But true to the saga of the project, nothing about that day was easy. The October weather was gray and miserable. Governor Thompson could not be flown into nearby Viroqua or Hillsboro municipal airstrips due to dense fog. I had never talked to the governor directly, but when his chief of staff called to tell us they couldn't fly in, I pleaded with him to consider alternatives, given the importance of the looming deadline. Then Governor Tommy Thompson got on the phone, and he didn't mince words over his "concern" about flying in this weather. As a friend from the Department of Transportation told me later, you're not a true public servant until you get the f-bomb dropped on you by the governor.

Fortunately, the fog was limited to the Kickapoo Valley, so with less than two hours notice, the representatives of the Ho-Chunk Nation, the state of Wisconsin, the Corps of Engineers, and the KRMB consortium and I made the one-hour drive to the La Crosse airport. The signatures were secured in a small room adjacent to the runway. This was not the celebration the groups had hoped for, but it was an incredible accomplishment everyone was proud to be a part of, and there was a huge sigh of relief that it was done.

In retrospect, the significance of bipartisanship throughout the political process at the federal and state levels is worth noting here too. Elected officials and their staff were more interested in finding a solution to a nagging problem for their constituents than in partisan one-upmanship. They were also willing to take a risk in working with the Ho-Chunk Nation, just as the Nation was willing to risk working with the state of Wisconsin and citizens in the valley. I'm not sure this would hold true if the Kickapoo Valley Reserve were proposed in our current hyper-partisan political climate.

7
Meanders

The Water Resources Development Act's requirement that the U.S. Army Corps of Engineers (COE) complete the remaining highway construction associated with the former La Farge Lake and Dam project was very important to most residents but not welcomed by all. COE staff made it clear that they were not in the business of building highways, so this was viewed as an added and odd burden for their work. They contracted through the State Department of Transportation (DOT) to oversee the design and construction of State Highway 131 and County Highways P and F.

As part of the La Farge Dam project, the COE had redesigned State Highway 131 between La Farge and Ontario and worked with the Wisconsin DOT to complete the construction of a five-mile segment of the new highway between La Farge and Rockton. (Otherwise, the original highway would have been at the bottom of the lake.) When the project was halted in 1975, so was the highway work.

The valley and its residents were left with one section of a well-designed new highway—including the legendary Rockton Bridge, a massive bridge originally designed to cross a lake but that now looks out of place, spanning the narrow Kickapoo River eighty feet below. The original six-mile section from Rockton to Ontario was still in need of repair. This stretch of highway included seven ancient bridges—some of which were one lane—and pavement that was crumbling due to age and frequent inundation from flooding.

In addition to mandating this section of Highway 131 be reconstructed, WRDA required that the portions of County Highways P and F within the project area be redone as well. Given the significantly altered purpose of the property, the hope was the new highway construction would have less of an impact on the environment. Had the new highway skirting the proposed lake been completed, a large swath would have run through the Bridge 8 Woods, which is a large contiguous block of forest important to the diverse and unique habitats of the property. Keeping the highway design primarily on the existing footprint avoided such a significant impact.

The newly required highway construction was another opportunity for community input and cooperation between state and federal agencies and the Ho-Chunk Nation. DOT representatives met repeatedly with various interest groups and agencies and modified the proposed highway design to avoid archeological sites and especially sensitive environmental areas. Some of these changes were heavily scrutinized due to the accompanying increase in costs or added details needed in construction design, but they survived.

The highway design concessions included the following:

- Building two land bridges—bridges spanning dry land instead of water—which reduced impacts to wetlands and other sensitive habitats.
- Constructing curved bridges to avoid impacting adjacent rock outcroppings.
- Installing small ledges under the bridge decking for nesting cliff swallows.
- Creating new wetlands at a three-to-one-acre ratio to mitigate those areas impacted by the highway. (An engineer described redrawing the footprint of the highway as "threading the needle" when he had to avoid an archeological site to the west and a wooded wetland to the east at one particularly tricky thirty-yard section.)
- Requiring the new bridges to have a decorative sandstone color and pattern that blended in with the surroundings since they would be viewed by thousands of river users floating underneath them.

- Requiring that native grasses, flowers, and trees be planted on the road banks following construction.
- Establishing a paved shoulder for bike safety and a speed limit of 45 miles per hour to slow the traffic on the curves.

A vocal minority challenged the first EIS on this new highway design because of the construction's possible impact on existing rural traffic, since semitrucks would be able to use the new bridges. But the overwhelming majority of local governments, valley residents, and agencies—including the Kickapoo Reserve Management Board—supported the highway reconstruction and recognized the delicate balance between road safety and environmental impacts.

If the MOU process taught me patience, the highway reconstruction process helped me to grow a thicker skin. Members of the highway reconstruction opposition group sent emails to environmental organization leaders I had worked with for years who accused me of "caving" to the DOT pressure and not protecting the environment. It was hard not to take this personally. Participating in countless meetings and discussions with the design engineers, it was clear to me they had made modifications as best they could while still meeting safety standards. I felt like we had to face the reality that roads have an environmental impact no matter how well-designed.

The final EIS described in detail the sensitive sites at risk of being impacted by the new construction and outlined the modifications being made to mitigate these impacts wherever possible. This EIS was approved and withstood a court challenge from those opposing the highway reconstruction. One member of the opposition was later arrested when she chained herself to a bulldozer the day construction was scheduled to start. Local papers devoted more ink to the progress of the construction than to this tactic that seemed straight out of *The Monkey Wrench Gang*.

The segment of County Highway P in need of reconstruction turned into a negotiation in itself, as the segment south of Rockton was susceptible to repeated flooding and included the beautiful but aged Bridge 13. After additional discussion, the county proposed transferring the existing segment to the state via the Kickapoo Reserve Management Board and constructing a new segment to intersect with Highway 131 south of Jug Creek. Again, it was tough to support new impacts on the property, but the long-term solution made sense. The swap also allowed the Old 131 multiuse recreation trail to be completed by linking Rockton to the south boundary of the Reserve, creating a roughly five-mile scenic segment for visitors to enjoy by biking, horseback riding, hiking, or cross-country skiing.

Additional opportunities to advocate for the Reserve continued to emerge. As the local utility—Vernon Electric Cooperative—planned for the highway construction phase, the KRMB and I requested the power lines be laid underground to protect the viewshed. As visitors enter from the north, they should see the beauty of the valley, not the poles and wires at the intersection of Highway 131 and County Road F. I had enough experience through my previous work with the Federation of Cooperatives to know it technically could be done, but I needed to put the justification together for it to be fiscally feasible. A reduction in brush removal and protection from storm damage was the best we could do. It was a long shot, and the contractor's installation experience was limited, but eventually, the electric cooperative agreed. Years later, when internet broadband cables were installed, the utility paralleled the electric power route and, in some segments, encased the lines together for easier repairs or replacement in the future. Although not seeing wires in the northern half of the Reserve is a subtle difference, it adds to the sense of a more remote property.

Money, Money, Money

As challenging as it was to get the new highway plan and the EIS approved, obtaining the funding for the mandated highway reconstruction and other work proved to be equally difficult. Although the Water Resources Development Act of 1996 authorized up to $17 million in federal funds for the construction, securing the actual appropriation of these funds turned out to be an annual struggle.

The COE had no incentive to include the project in their annual budget requests, given their ever-growing obligations nationwide for flood control and dam repair projects. Each year, the Wisconsin congressional delegation and their staff proposed funding based on requests I'd write on behalf of the KRMB and Wisconsin state officials. Fortunately, 7th District Congressman David Obey, chair of the prestigious House Appropriations Committee at the time, and newly elected 3rd District Congressman Ron Kind understood the struggles the area had experienced and recognized the need to get the work done. Senators Russ Feingold and Herb Kohl continued to champion the project on the Senate side and defended the funding as the federal budget bills worked through the approval process. Governor Tommy Thompson, State Senator Brian Rude, State Representative DuWayne Johnsrud, and the Ho-Chunk Nation leaders also contacted their influential friends in D.C. to ensure the funding came through each year from 1997 to 2002.

Highway reconstruction began in 2001 and was completed in August 2003. A ceremonial ribbon cutting was held at Bridge 7. Afterward, celebratory refreshments were enjoyed at Rockton Bar, which featured an interesting mix of construction workers, elected officials, Ho-Chunk Nation members, DOT staff, KRMB members, and me. Stories of the challenges and triumphs were eye-opening and punctuated with fun anecdotes. Similar to the process with the MOU, everyone was happy to have been involved—and even happier that it was done.

Soliciting Public Input

Early in my tenure, it became apparent that I had at least two major strikes against me: I wasn't born and raised in the Kickapoo Valley, and I wasn't a man. Since I couldn't change those two facts, I tried to make the best of both issues. Newcomers to this area will learn quickly that the label of outsider lasts forever. However, not being local allowed me to ask more questions about everyone and everything. I wasn't playing dumb; I was a blank slate. The majority of residents simply wanted me to know their story or why they felt connected to the property. Even though I would have been considered a bureaucrat through employment, I was now their resident bureaucrat.

The KRMB members recognized the importance of ongoing citizen input and assigned a couple of subcommittees to report regularly on issues of land management and next steps. Subcommittees were especially important to me, as we utilized the opportunity to get members from various interests to participate in the solution. More directly, those who complained about or criticized the process were invited to serve on a committee to help figure out a solution. Formally making them committee members allowed each of us to understand the concerns or limitations much better.

Even before the MOU was approved, we all recognized that fulfilling the requirement in the WRDA for the COE to clean up the property would be exceptionally challenging given the size, years of vegetative growth, and difficult terrain. Although homes, barns, and other buildings had been moved or torn down to make way for the dam and lake, the common practice of each previous homestead having its own dump for trash, abandoned vehicles, mink cages, and other equipment was evident on the land. Clearly, the thought of everything being at the bottom of the proposed lake had allowed for lots of latitude in the 1970s. In addition, there wasn't the understanding of the environmental impacts of everything from waste oil at car repair shops to asbestos products from the buildings. Even a former shooting range used for target practice raised the awareness of lead contamination in the soil. And, as previously mentioned, when there was no on-site management of the property, people threw appliances and tires in the ravines; even abandoned cars were found on some sites.

Members of the KRMB subcommittee knew those sites better than I could have ever hoped to. Combining their list with some sites the archeological inventory group had literally stumbled upon gave us a lengthy catalog of sites the COE would be responsible for cleaning up.

Although their hearts may have been in the right place, the COE staff were often put in unfortunate situations when it came to dealing with local residents and sticking to the federal directive and budget. The monthly KRMB meetings became an opportunity for the COE project manager to provide updates on the transfer process, to which the board members and often the citizens or local press in attendance would offer immediate feedback. Common sense eventually prevailed, but it took persistence to resolve the challenges encountered with many of the sites and develop a shared understanding of what the cleanup would mean.

The most visible example of this is the 110-foot concrete water control tower located east of the incomplete dam berm. Depending on how the Water Resources Development Act is interpreted, the tower could have been removed as part of the cleanup effort. It had become a liability as teens and young adults had discovered an access to a great overlook and party spot through the center of the tower via a ladder. A COE representative estimated that it would cost $164,000 (significant money in 1999) to dismantle and dispose of the massive structure. Local headlines and community discussions during the monthly board meetings led me to plan a public input session specific to the tower and create a survey of residents' preferences.

The overwhelming majority felt the tower should stay standing and not one more penny should be spent on that symbol of the boondoggle. A compromise was negotiated, and the COE contracted with a local scrap dealer to remove the copper, metal, and lead from the interior of the tower and permanently close the entry with concrete. With the liability problem solved, the tower now stands as an educational symbol of how close the Kickapoo River was to being blocked by a dam.

A contract was issued for the lengthy list of other cleanup sites in the formal federal process. The winning bidder was not from the valley, and although the land was being mapped with the latest GIS technology at the time, accuracy of the locations was sometimes a challenge. The Ho-Chunk Nation staff, subcommittee members, or other residents would regularly accompany the cleanup crew to the sites on the list. As work progressed, we'd make sure one of us or the COE staff would check to make sure it was done correctly and completely. More than once, they'd get called back out to a remote site or ravine to get objects they missed or maybe chose not to see. Slowly but surely, all the sites we had listed were completed. Again, the feeling of progress was shared, and the community had a real sense that their input made a visual difference on the landscape.

Dealing with the flowing wells on the property was another interesting challenge. If you're not familiar with groundwater wells, the science is simple, but the results are somewhat magical and revered as culturally significant. This region is peppered with natural springs—water bubbling up from underground. Early settlers recognized the benefit and pressurized the natural springs with casings and pipes to force the water up higher and directly to their barns for watering livestock and nearer their houses for ease of access. The water flows nonstop 365 days per year. Throughout the area, residents have come to know which water tastes the best and which wells have too much iron or sulfur, which ruins the taste. Many folks credit their longevity and good health to drinking the water from these wells.

Environmentally, the springs are critical to supplying wetland areas with a constant source of water to support the variety of plants, insects, amphibians, and birds the KRMB was now directed to protect. Therefore, the remaining flowing wells at former homesteads that had not been previously abandoned when the COE purchased the property generated a great deal of discussion. Wisconsin's DNR is authorized to enforce codes dealing with wells, and in 1997 it inspected fourteen wells. The result was the proper abandonment of eight wells, which entailed a licensed well driller pulling the pipe and removing the casing. Depending on the flow, the water would simply percolate elsewhere. Or, if removal of the pressure left a hole, the well was sealed with bentonite. The remaining flowing wells were to be upgraded and clearly marked not for human consumption because they could not be tested frequently enough to guarantee potable water. Many residents found that to be amusing since they'd been consuming it their whole lives with no ill effects.

The flowing wells at the campsites known as Potts Corners, Ma & Pa's Park, and Hay Valley are the most visible to the public and still flow strong. One of my favorite emails in the early years was from a visitor who happened upon the campsite at Potts Corners and shared that they had a wonderful weekend visiting the Reserve. They did, however, feel compelled to write and express concern that we were wasting water by allowing that faucet to run 24/7 and recommended adding a shutoff valve. The email was rather lengthy, chiding me about how precious water is to our planet and the need to conserve it. I had a good laugh about the scolding and enjoyed replying with some flowery wording on the natural wonders of water, why springs exist throughout the Kickapoo Valley, and how it was impossible for me to shut the water off.

8
Tandem Paddling

It is historically significant that the memorandum of understanding and management plan were agreed upon by the state of Wisconsin and the Ho-Chunk Nation, with implementation through the Kickapoo Reserve Management Board (KRMB). But it is even more notable that this relationship has successfully survived for more than two decades, as a sovereign nation and an entity of state government share a common mission to protect, preserve, and enhance the Kickapoo Valley Reserve's unique environmental, scenic, and cultural features while providing opportunities for the use and enjoyment of visitors.

From my introductory meeting with tribal leaders in 1996, when I relayed my childhood interactions with the Oneida Tribe of the Green Bay area and was gently redirected and informed about the Ho-Chunk Nation ancestors of that region, I have climbed a steep learning curve about tribal history. The curriculum used when I was in grade school was woefully inadequate when it came to learning about the people who were here long before white settlers.

For instance, it was during the negotiations for the Memorandum of Understanding (MOU) when I heard about the importance of clans within the tribe, and I learned that each of the twelve clans in the Ho-Chunk Nation has a primary role recognized through family structure and duty: those who are above (Thunder, Warrior, Eagle, and Pigeon), and those who are on earth (Bear, Buffalo, Deer, Wolf, Elk, Fish, Water Spirit, and Snake). Each of these clans is entrusted with distinct responsibilities, such as judicial matters, health and safety, and civic responsibilities. Knowing this, I could better understand why every time we thought we were making progress in drafting the MOU and joint management plan, a Ho-Chunk Nation staff member would indicate that a member and/or elder of another clan would need to review and approve a revision prior to the Nation's acceptance.

Even the tribal name of Ho-Chunk required repeated explanations at public meetings and day-to-day encounters in the community. The name *Ho-Chunk* loosely translates to "People of the Big Voice." Prior to the adoption of a new tribal constitution in 1994, the Ho-Chunk people were known as the Wisconsin Winnebago. *Winnebago* is said to be a botched translation by white explorers of an unflattering reference used by the neighboring Sac and Fox tribes that implies "people of the dirty waters," which is a reference to the waters of Lake Winnebago and the Fox River that became brown and weedy in the heat of the summer.

The Ho-Chunk Historic Preservation Department provided the MOU negotiating team with a sixteen-page historical timeline to help them understand the tribe's history. The "Ho-Chunk (Wisconsin Winnebago) Chronology" begins in 1634 with Jean Nicolet meeting the Winnebago in the Green Bay area and continues up to 1995 when the Ho-Chunk Nation moved into its new administrative headquarters building in Black River Falls. The respected anthropologist Nancy Oestreich Lurie of UW–Milwaukee also provided a variety of documents and direct communication to the state members of the negotiating team that proved invaluable in understanding the profound connection Native Americans have to their ancestral homeland.

It is interesting to note that, unlike the Sioux, Fox, and Kickapoo, who were also linked to southwest Wisconsin and were removed by the U.S. Army, the Ho-Chunk Nation ancestors repeatedly returned to their ancestral lands throughout central and southwest Wisconsin. When the question of other tribes' historical connections with the Kickapoo Valley land emerged during the negotiations on the MOU, one of the Ho-Chunk elders explained that given the painful history of the treaties and how white men used political boundaries instead of nature's boundaries, the Ho-Chunk Nation as the People of the

Big Voice would represent the hearts and minds of all the tribes who had previously walked the Kickapoo Valley. At one point during negotiations, representatives of the Kickapoo Tribe traveled from their headquarters in McLoud, Oklahoma, to visit the property and meet with representatives from the state, the U.S. Army Corps of Engineers, and the Ho-Chunk Nation. Following the visit, they asked to be provided with copies of the agreements once completed, but there was no indication they wanted to formally participate in the process.

As the negotiations rode the roller coaster between requests for postponing the land transfer and suggestions the tribe hold out for the entire 8,600 acres, protecting the land became the repeated mantra that smoothed emotions and allowed agreements to emerge. Everyone in the meetings listened as elders and elected leaders of the Nation talked about their deeply held beliefs that the plan for the KVR should look seven generations ahead and how we are all "of the Earth"—that every living thing has a soul, and Earth Mother is in every blade of grass and acorn on this protected area. Everyone then would agree that protection was the highest priority. Our eye-to-eye agreement on this seemed more important than any words on paper, but we had to document everything for the federal and state governments.

Throughout the negotiations, clan affiliation and discussions about who could or could not speak on behalf of the tribe appeared to be competitive infighting. At one of the meetings, an elder shared a traditional story about how tribal members can sometimes be like a pot of lobsters. As the heat of the water rises and a few lobsters try to climb out, the other lobsters will pull them back down rather than let any survive.

I was also privileged to witness events when tribal members came together in good and bad times. It was an honor to be invited to a traditional funeral held for John Blackdeer, a tribal member who had died too young. We had come to know him through surveys of the property and appreciated his quick wit and charisma. During the services, other tribal members patiently explained to me the rituals and John's interwoven family connections. Members of each clan paid tribute to John with prayers, songs, and a drum circle, and they provided the feast for the ceremony. In mourning, the clans were united.

Whenever I got frustrated with any aspect of the joint management being held up by changes in tribal leadership or clan representation, I reminded myself that the tribal structure is somewhat like my eight siblings: we may squabble at times, but when it comes to the important stuff, we are family.

I have developed a much clearer understanding of and empathy with the Ho-Chunk Nation as I learned more of the tribe's history and challenges and the tenacity of these proud people. Apart from my KVR work, I've come to know a member of the Ho-Chunk Nation, with whom I had a heartfelt discussion about what she and her family have endured. I told her of an impulse I've had many times in meetings over the years to apologize to tribal members for what our ancestors and our current culture have done. But she replied that every group, race, and religion have endured hardships created by another, and Native peoples are not unique in their struggle to continue their traditions or tell their stories accurately. "What is important," she said, "is to listen to the stories and learn not to repeat the mistakes of the past."

An Arranged Marriage Takes Work

The official dedication ceremony and celebration held on May 11, 2001, on the site of what would become the Kickapoo Valley Reserve Visitor Center had threads of symbolism reminiscent of a wedding. Although the state portion of land had been transferred from federal ownership in December 2000, the interagency transfer from the Corps of Engineers to the BIA in trust for the Ho-Chunk Nation was completed on-site that day, and the Kickapoo Valley residents and the Ho-Chunk Nation were now formally committed to each other in managing the property.

Parallels to what the displaced residents and the Ho-Chunk Nation ancestors had been through were obvious. The Ho-Chunk ancestors and the descendants of white settlers had both been removed from this land, and it was now returned for them to care for on behalf of the public. Especially touching was the scene of elders from each group seated next to each other and sharing stories about the hard work of putting up tobacco in their youth and how they were looking forward to the spring fishing season. It was quickly clear that the two groups had more in common than they had thought.

As with most weddings, the party was fun to plan, but the marriage would take work. The evolution of the agreement did not start with cooperation; had the 1994 federal legislation passed, the Ho-Chunk Nation would have had no formal involvement. Had the 1996 WRDA failed, the Ho-Chunk Nation might have been managing the entire 8,600 acres. But now the state of Wisconsin, Kickapoo Valley residents, and the Ho-Chunk Nation were entwined and committed to the future of the project.

Figuring out how the joint management would actually work was made easier by the fact that representatives of the KRMB and Ho-Chunk Nation staff members had developed good working relationships during the two years prior to the transfer. Searching for survey markers to establish accurate boundaries could only be done on foot in small groups, and nothing builds trust quite like walking together through prickly ash and briars to find a marker or helping each other balance on a log to cross a cold-water creek. Meeting for lunch over a burger and comparing notes about what was found or inventoried helped to bring everyone together, and exchanging stories of what was in dump sites evolved into a shared goal of making sure every nasty site was on the list for the COE to clean up. Nobody wanted to inherit those.

Per the 1995 proposal from Ho-Chunk Nation President Chloris Lowe Jr., documented in the MOU in 1999, the state of Wisconsin had agreed to add two members from the Ho-Chunk Nation to the KRMB. From the state's perspective, this was an olive branch that demonstrated sincerity and trust in the partnership. Representation on the board was important to the Ho-Chunk Nation elders and legislators to ensure they would have input in decisions for the future of the land. Members were nominated directly by the Ho-Chunk Nation president and their legislators with the Wisconsin governor's official appointment only a formality. Having two members formally participating and voting on future policies for the property confirmed the Ho-Chunk Nation's role in joint management for the entire 8,600 acres.

Equally significant to future cooperation was the promise to protect archeological sites throughout the property. Including penalties in the administrative rules for the 7,400 acres owned by the state of Wisconsin proved the KRMB was serious about this protection. The illegal market for artifacts motivates looting, and sadly, many of the burial mounds within and just south of the Reserve had been looted prior to the transfer. Though the Wisconsin Historical Society had been accused of ransacking artifacts by tribes in some situations, it had archived some of the objects found in the 1970s during the initial surveys while assuming the area would be inundated with water for the lake. In hindsight, this might have protected the artifacts from theft, and they were displayed for public education in the KVR Visitor Center exhibits with the Ho-Chunk Nation's approval.

How to deal with artifacts has always been a sensitive subject. Early on in my tenure, I was told the story of two archaeologists who were contracted to survey the Highway 131 reroute from La Farge to Rockton in the early 1970s. Legend has it they authorized the highway construction to go through a significant archeological site. Soon after construction equipment tore the site apart, the two archaeologists were killed in a car accident on their way to their next survey site in Iowa. I didn't take the time to research the story, and I felt I didn't need to. Sites are to be protected because it's the right thing to do, and I'm not going to be the one to authorize anything that would test the powers of spirits, ghosts, or any other invisible forces.

Over the years, people would bring in buckets of arrowheads they'd found in their fields or other areas. Spring tilling would bring the items to the surface. Some were obviously discarded materials, as if the hunter simply broke a tip in the process of making it. Although the visitor may have thought they'd brought us a treasure, it was my job to politely decline the donation. It would have been impossible to properly display, archive, or find storage space for the volume of pieces.

One of the early frustrations following the land transfer was how to truly ensure its protection. State legislation authorized the KRMB to have its own police enforcement, but it did not authorize hiring an employee to enforce the policies and rules. The KRMB had to formally request a position be created and funded. Jurisdictional issues with tribal laws complicated the implementation even further. Sovereign nations normally have their own enforcement and judicial process. Should someone be arrested on trust land by officers reporting to the KRMB, it was not clear if this would hold up in the Ho-Chunk Nation or state systems. Oh, how I wished I had gone to law school so I could better understand the intricacies of mutual aid, liability, and jurisdiction.

Fortunately, I was able to draft the concept in plain language, and the state attorneys assigned to the KVR put it into legalese for us. A compromise was reached by contracting through the Vernon County Sheriff's Department with an understanding that allowed for enforcement on both trust and state lands within the county. Later, officers assigned specifically to the Reserve were hired, and an agreement was forged with county dispatch to cover issues anywhere within the property. Funding through the state gaming appropriation was suggested by the Ho-Chunk Nation legislative liaison. Each tribe operating casinos in the state contributes to the Gaming Fund through an assessment negotiated in each tribe's gaming compact. The fee is similar to a sales tax, and each tribe identifies priorities for the appropriation in the state of Wisconsin's biannual budget process. In the case of the KVR, the appropriation supports 25 percent of a full-time property manager who is also certified in law enforcement, the part-time officers hired to patrol the property, and the equipment needed to do so.

Joint Management in Practice

After the official land transfer, the work of labeling boundaries and making accurate maps became a high priority. The two blocks making up the Ho-Chunk Nation trust lands had to be identified by the maps provided to the public as directed by the state legislation, but on the property itself, there were intentionally no clear markers differentiating the state-owned land from trust lands. Survey markers are the only indication of boundaries, and those markers are rarely visible to trail users due to vegetation or snow cover. This approach helped to quell rumors of fenced-off areas and other restrictions on land use. The average visitor does not know what to look for in terms of archeological sites, so the best protection for sites was the hands-off approach of having an educational brochure explaining archeological significance but not indicating exact locations.

Turnover of leadership in the Ho-Chunk Nation brought new management challenges rather frequently. During my twenty-four-year tenure, the Ho-Chunk Nation elected twelve presidents. Even though the tribe's constitution provides for four-year terms, some presidents have served only one or two years. Each new president would appoint new staff members in leadership roles for the Nation's Departments of Natural Resources and Heritage Preservation—the departments we worked with most often. If the new staff members were not aware of existing agreements, surprises were sure to follow.

That was the case in September 2001, when a neighbor to the Reserve asked us who was logging in the Black Hawk Rock area. Surprised by this news, I went to see for myself and found a crew of three men from the Ho-Chunk Nation cutting trees along the western edge of the trust land in that quadrant. They indicated that their boss told them to start clearing timber as the tribe was going to erect a fence around the trust land. In addition, no trespassing signs had been erected. This was a clear violation of the MOU. I fired off a very blunt email to the attorney for the Ho-Chunk Nation we had worked with throughout the negotiations. Within two days, the signs were removed, and the tree clearing stopped, but sadly, some beautiful oak trees were lost due to the incident.

Another memorable surprise was when an employee of the Ho-Chunk Nation who managed the buffalo herd at a Ho-Chunk property an hour south of us stopped by the office to ask for directions to the Ho-Chunk land. He was there to assess which fields could be used for grazing bison. Grazing had been discussed during the initial negotiations but quickly dismissed due to the anticipated problem of maintaining fences and the potential risks to both the animals and visitors if they interacted. Another near miss, but no bison are on the Reserve as of this writing.

The importance of communication between the KRMB, the Ho-Chunk Nation leadership, and their respective staff was illustrated repeatedly. Built into the MOU and management plan is a five-year review process that triggers the KRMB to review the original management plan and send a letter to the president of the Ho-Chunk Nation and the governor of the state of Wisconsin confirming that the agreements are being implemented and highlighting programs and projects of mutual benefit. If the MOU symbolizes a marriage, these five-year reviews are a renewal of vows. It was my job to make sure the board and the Ho-Chunk Nation leadership took an active part in this review. Pestering everyone with emails and letters of request to make sure the tribal staff takes the list of goals and accomplishments through the chain of command for approval is tedious but always worth it. It serves as a reminder to each entity how unique and important our arrangement is for the river and the land of the Reserve.

Management of the 1,200 acres of trust land has evolved as the tribe's Natural Resources Division has developed and gained experience with their properties throughout the state. In addition, the BIA and its trained network of staff based in Ashland, Wisconsin, provide personnel, equipment, and funding to assist tribes in the Midwest. Land management practices such as prescribed burns on prairie restoration sites demonstrate the cooperative work between the BIA and the Ho-Chunk Nation. Water quality testing, forest inventory data, and recreational trail restorations have been the result of cooperative work. The tribe is also working with the locally headquartered Organic Valley Cooperative to convert agricultural fields on the trust land to meet organic standards. Funding through the BIA enabled the Ho-Chunk Nation Roads Division to restore a historic bridge, construct two covered trail bridges, and replace a section of asphalt on the Old 131 Trail segment adjacent to the southern block of trust land—a multimillion-dollar project that would not have been possible through the limited KRMB budget.

For the most part, the KVR staff does the day-to-day work, like mowing or clearing fallen trees from the trails. Special projects, such as the Weister Creek habitat work, segments of trail reconstruction, tree planting, and special event-related tasks evolve via the monthly KRMB meetings or through the goals and objectives from the corresponding Finance, Land Management, Education, and Tourism Plans. Ho-Chunk Nation staff are invited to participate in meetings and edit the plans prior to board approval. Any trail rerouting or repair, and any campsite or restoration project that requires digging into the soil at a depth of fourteen inches or more, triggers the need for a formal archeological survey prior to starting.

Over the years, contracts with the Mississippi Valley Archeology Center at the University of Wisconsin–La Crosse that follow State Historic Preservation Office procedures and are approved by the Ho-

Chunk Nation's tribal historic preservation officer have helped to ensure that cultural sites are protected from construction impacts as much as possible. Unfortunately, exposure to the elements, such as the weathering of sandstone where petroglyphs were carved or the repeated flooding of traditional village campsites, is beyond the scope of protection.

Communication, learning from experience, and a shared sense of taking care of the land have allowed this agreement to continue to work. During the negotiations for the MOU and as the management plans developed, Ho-Chunk Nation members repeatedly referenced the need to think seven generations ahead, just as their elders had during the negotiations for the transfer. This awareness keeps future generations in mind when we are planning to plant prairies and oaks or reroute a trail. Would whatever we are planning help or hinder future generations' ability to care for the land? Will the land still be preserved and protected 175 years from now? As in any marriage, it will take work and commitment to achieve the long-term goals.

Opportunity to Accurately Educate

The education program is vital to the overall success of the KVR. Consistently through the years and included in the original proposal of 1993 from the Citizen Advisory Committee, the MOU, and the master and management plans, an education program was recognized as an asset to the project and the surrounding communities.

The unique management agreement with the Ho-Chunk Nation was an unprecedented opportunity to provide programming specific to Native American history, culture, and current land management practices. Some members within the tribe still question the ability of non-Indigenous people to teach their history, since stories, beliefs, and descriptions of historic events are traditionally passed down orally from tribal elders to the next generation. Discussions can seem very circular when tribal members point out the poor job school systems do in teaching Indigenous people's history while at the same time being unwilling to share their oral history or explain how the instructors could teach it in the KVR setting. Some tribal members will share only as much as they want to share and only when they want to share it. In practice, the trust of an individual and institution needs to be built first.

Early attempts to have a written curriculum approved by the Ho-

Chunk Nation cultural representatives went unanswered. Eventually, board member Bill Quackenbush, who serves as the tribal historic preservation officer for the Ho-Chunk Nation, was a featured speaker at the annual instructor training that helped establish certain ground rules for the education program, which allowed KVR instructors to teach visiting students about the history of tribes as hunters and gatherers in the Kickapoo River region. In 2010, Bill provided instructions and guided a group of volunteers on how to construct a *ciporoke* near the visitor center, a replica of the traditional housing their ancestors used in this region. The model was not entirely authentic because twine and plastic tarp were used in the construction instead of traditional woven fibers and animal hides. Nevertheless, the oblong tent served as a unique outdoor classroom for KVR instructors to describe how and why the Native peoples would construct a temporary dwelling as they moved through the valley during the summer seasons but would utilize sturdier rock shelters or go to village gathering sites to share food, shelter, and supplies during the winter months.

Shared management of the property has also allowed the KVR to enhance and expand opportunities for non-Native visitors to attend special events in which representatives of the Ho-Chunk Nation participate. During the KVR's annual winter festival, storytelling is offered in the ciporoke. People of all ages are greeted with the scent of burning smudge sticks or traditional herbs as they sit on hay bale-braced benches. The wood burner, although less authentic than the open fire of their ancestors, keeps them warm while a tribal member dressed in a traditional beaded animal-skin shirt and accessories shares mesmerizing sagas about the Native people's intimate connection to the land, waters, flora, fauna, and seasons. These successful programs are both informational and entertaining, and stereotypes are often addressed directly during the question-and-answer sessions that follow the presentation. The images of "Indians" depicted in old television westerns or films such as *Dances with Wolves* give way to more respectful and accurate portraits at these in-person events.

In addition, instructors for the KVR meet with representatives of the Ho-Chunk Nation to better understand what is and isn't appropriate to discuss about the tribe's history and sacred sites. The Ho-Chunk Nation's education department also utilizes the property for their language immersion classes and the sharing of oral history and ceremonial traditions. These classes are held near the recognized ceremonial site known to us as Black Hawk Rock—although the tribe has another name for it. My understanding is this particular rock outcropping is where a young man could carry out a vision quest by fasting and staying in solitude for a period of time to allow spiritual direction into adulthood.

This remote location allows the instructors to eliminate distractions for the students. No video games or cell phones are allowed, and the option for hikes to a magnificent view on top of an important ceremonial site no doubt increases the impact of the young tribal members' experience.

The Ho-Chunk Nation's sponsorship of various fundraising events for the KVR education program is also noteworthy. The annual Dam Challenge Triathlon and Winter Fest benefit from the Nation's financial contributions, in-kind materials, and staff labor. For many years, a beautiful woven blanket donated to the Friends of the KVR for the annual auction would bring the highest bids of all items.

In 2022, efforts to upgrade the exhibits in the visitor center focused attention on a more accurate depiction of all the tribes who have utilized the Kickapoo River Valley, including the namesake Kickapoo Tribe, as this was the last known place their people were united as one tribe before being split up between Kansas, Oklahoma, and Texas. The upgrade expands the description of why and how the Ho-Chunk Nation and the state of Wisconsin are managing the KVR project together and illustrates the language of the tribe in each panel description.

Aids in Lieu of Taxes on Trust Land

The MOU and the management plan used soft language—*may* instead of *must*—when it came to addressing local municipalities' concerns over the equivalent of property tax payments on the 1,200 acres of trust lands. Item 8 in the 1997 MOU states: "In balance with the State responsibility, the Nation may agree to pay a sum sufficient in lieu of taxes to the local government directly affected by the placement of lands into trust located within their geographical boundary."

In 2008, the state of Wisconsin and the Ho-Chunk Nation

renegotiated the tribe's gaming compact. Compacts are required for all tribes that offer gaming in the state, and the Ho-Chunk Nation was then operating three casinos located in Wisconsin Dells, Black River Falls, and Madison. Contained within the 2008 amendment was language allowing the tribe to be credited for payments made to counties that contained trust lands at a rate of $1,000 per acre. I received a call from a friend in Madison who was familiar with the gaming compact details, which made me aware of the specific language. I, in turn, called the Vernon County treasurer.

In another example of bipartisanship, the Vernon County treasurer and county board chairman were active in the Republican party, and Democrat Governor Jim Doyle's administration negotiated the compact. Rightfully so, the Vernon County officials verified my news via their trusted allies at the Wisconsin Counties Association. In 2010, annual payments of $1.2 million to Vernon County began in recognition of the 1,200 acres of trust land within the Reserve. This additional revenue is an important part of the budget for one of the poorest counties in the state. The county, in turn, transfers some of the money to the towns of Stark and Whitestown, where the property is located, as aids in lieu of taxes. More than one Ho-Chunk Nation member has pointed out the irony of the white man's system of government that expects payment for lands requiring few, if any, services when no compensation was given during the historical removal of tribes from land they considered their home.

Over the years, the local rumors about the Ho-Chunk Nation "land grab" have quieted considerably. Residents feared (or hoped) a casino would be built on the property, but that was never part of the formal negotiation. The tribe's three casinos are strategically located along interstate highways and near population centers for access to more customers and a bigger workforce pool. The payment to the county government has further illustrated the tribe's commitment to supporting the local area. During one of the early public planning meetings, a descendant of a former landowner stated the land should have been "returned to the original owners." Ritchie Brown of the Ho-Chunk Nation was seated next to me and quietly commented that he would agree but had a different opinion on who the "original" landowners were.

Stereotypes persist, and at times I have been embarrassed by them and guilty of acting on them myself. One personally cringeworthy event occurred when a local resident asked me to put him in touch with a Ho-Chunk Nation member for a photo shoot on the trust lands. I assumed he wanted to go up to Black Hawk Rock and photograph the panoramic view, but I was wrong. This guy wanted to create a throwback to the "Wild West" in the Kickapoo Valley to advertise a business he was planning to open. He had the Ho-Chunk member sit bareback on a horse, shirtless, with his long black hair blowing in the wind and the vacant land as a backdrop. When the tribal member told me what had happened, I apologized profusely, but he responded with good humor. "It's okay. I made sure to get paid cash before I got on that horse."

9
Watershed Moments

The intersection of political action and citizen activism is a consistent thread in the evolution of the Kickapoo Valley Reserve (KVR). Citizen activism initiated the dam and lake project for the benefit of the community, and the community eventually reacted to the project's demise by initiating the creation of the KVR for the benefit of all.

Although many community members had been impacted by the loss of private land for the dam project, going forward, the proposal to keep the land open to the public and ensure local involvement was supported by nearly all residents. The sense that distant bureaucrats and politicians had made decisions on the dam and lake made local control a high priority for the management board. Frustration and downright anger toward government entities like the U.S. Army Corps of Engineers (COE), the DNR, and various politicians are still expressed to this day. Environmental groups are often described with equal disdain. The Sierra Club was said to be the source of the negative media attention the project attracted. Residents were offended by hearing this area being compared to poverty-stricken Appalachia and being known only as the site of a government boondoggle. Board members, business owners, and local elected officials were ready to look toward the future instead of the past.

Wisconsin State Statute 41.41 also directed the KRMB to promulgate rules for the property—what is and is not allowed on the property—as well as address fees for use of the property and enforce penalties for rule violations. Clearly stated rules that are available to the public in a variety of formats have been vital to achieving the mission to preserve and protect. Obviously, not everyone likes being told what they can or can't do, but land managers cannot rely on common sense when it comes to protecting such an important property. The Legislative Reference Bureau staff guided me through the process of drafting the scope statement, holding public hearings, and submitting the statement to the state legislature.

The board and I used the DNR rules governing state parks and forests as a template rather than trying to reinvent the wheel in formulating public policy. But the flexibility for the stand-alone KRMB to go one step further than the DNR in protecting the land was evident from the details and penalties for the desecration of cultural and archeological sites within the property. Prohibiting the use of metal detectors and requiring research permits for archeological research and plant collection were simple but important preventative measures when it came to the day-to-day protection of sites.

The lawlessness on and damage to the "government land" from 1975 to 1996 also brought the community together in support of oversight. Ruts are still visible at the base of Black Hawk Rock, where trucks would be chained to a tree, driven as far up the steep slope as possible, then winched the rest of the way up. Off-roading on ATVs and horseback riding wherever and whenever the riders chose grew in popularity. Some people felt that these visitors were helping the economy by patronizing the gas stations, bars, and motels, but the community as a whole wasn't benefiting.

Rogue campers, such as the infamous Rainbow Family Gathering, were also unsettling to residents. Law enforcement and emergency personnel found it difficult to deal with large groups camping in remote settings. In brief, the Rainbow gatherings usually set up in remote areas of national forest property in early July and made the case that all residents owned the federal lands, so they had the right to be there. Although the annual gatherings have been held throughout the U.S., they selected the U.S. Army Corps of Engineers' land in 1992 and 1994. Whether accurate or exaggerated, stories of children begging for food, significant drug use, and reports of bounced checks at the local businesses were the talk of the town and local media. Impacts to the land included human waste issues and trampling of vegetation. The events made a lasting impression on community members and local law enforcement that would illustrate why the land and river would need some formal safeguards.

The Citizen Advisory Committee proposal had set a baseline by endorsing low-impact recreation for the property. The MOU and management plans went further by clearly articulating that there would be no motorized vehicle recreation except for snowmobiles using a trail inherited as part of the statewide trail system. These decisions set the stage for discussions regarding land use. Who would be allowed to use the land? Where would they be allowed? And how would the policies be enforced?

Simultaneous with the rule process, the KRMB invited and encouraged residents and recreationists to be involved as the board began creating a master plan for the property to answer these questions. Many user groups showed up and were not shy about expressing their opinions. One Saturday morning meeting in the spring of 1998 brought nearly 200 people out to a forum held at the La Farge public school. After hearing an update on the land transfer status and planning process, the participants were divided into groups under the guidance of trained facilitators from the Vernon County Extension Service. Relying on local facilitators added a layer of trust since most of them were familiar faces, and they followed the practice of good facilitation by encouraging courtesy and respect so every voice could be heard.

Of course, it was not all roses and olive branches. It seemed every potential user group, including some who hadn't been thought of, had their own ideas. Farmers, loggers, fishermen, hunters, canoers, horseback riders, bicyclists, ATV riders, snowmobilers, bird watchers, and morel mushroom hunters all spoke up. One participant wearing a ten-gallon cowboy hat and a long riding coat stood on the edge of a small group session and pulled his coat back a bit at the hip to make sure the facilitator and I knew he was wearing a holster and gun. Mountain bike enthusiasts were openly referred to as Mountain Dew Boys and horseback riders as Marlboro Men—terms that were not always used endearingly. The commitment people have to their recreational hobbies was on full display.

What came out of these sessions was a laundry list of activities for the KRMB to establish policy on and create rules to address. Some were easy and could be simply stated, like continuing to allow hunting and fishing in accordance with state seasons and laws. When a suggestion was made for trout fishing to be catch-and-release only, similar to what was allowed on the West Fork of the Kickapoo River, KRMB member Sandy Heidel defended the need for kids to have the experience of being able to catch a fish and cook it over an open fire streamside. "Then you have a fisherman for life." The strong tradition of public hunting and trapping on the land since the early 1970s would continue. Agriculture leases and harvesting of timber for revenue also had overwhelming support but with the added caveats requiring conservation practices on the cropped fields and the timber harvests to be sustainably managed.

Decisions about trail use proved to be more difficult. Over the years, horseback riders had ranged freely over the property. An unsustainable system of trails resembling a spaghetti plate had developed. Unfortunately, some of the most popular equestrian trails went over or through sensitive archeological and environmental sites. Due to a lack of planning, trails often went straight up steep slopes, which allowed for rain and snowmelt to erode the soil. When the ruts got too deep to ride in, a parallel ribbon of trails would develop. Given the extensive network of trails, an inventory needed to be done to evaluate their impact on significant sites. Our field staff and I worked with DNR biologists and staff and Ho-Chunk Nation mapping technicians on this evaluation. Some horseback riders were cooperative; others were not since the inventory would lead to changes in one of their favorite places to ride.

Determinations were made to close some of the trails outright. Most notable was the riders' access to Black Hawk Rock. The overlook is one of the most impressive views in the Reserve. It stands 1,203 feet above sea level with a visible rock surface 55 feet tall that provides a sweeping view to the west, south, and east. On a clear day, the village of La Farge is visible five miles away. The access to the overlook is rocky and steep. Experienced horseback riders have always loved it, but considerable damage to the site had already occurred. Given that the rock serves as a Ho-Chunk ceremonial site, it needed protection from further human impact. So equestrian access to the overlook was denied, although a hitching post was constructed near the base of the rock to allow riders to hike the most sensitive areas once their horse or mule was tied securely.

Early maps showed riders which designated trails were approved for equestrian use, but there was often fresh evidence of continued use on closed trails. Riders would staple paper plates to trees at intersections to show fellow riders where to follow the trails to their favorite destinations, and enforcement was nearly impossible in such a large tract of land.

An unfortunate incident in 2000 raised awareness of how serious this issue was. A group of riders were on a closed section of trail when a child was thrown off his mule and slid down an embankment above the river. When his grandfather tried to help, he got into trouble too. The only way the local emergency medical technicians could reach them and bring them out was by crossing the Kickapoo River in a flat-bottom rowboat. The grandfather's injuries were significant, and the two had to be flown to the hospital by helicopter. Safety would always be an issue in this remote setting, and having people riding along a cliff face over the river was not safe for the riders or the community of volunteer EMTs.

After the trail evaluations were completed, the following policies were developed to protect the land, vegetation, archeological sites, and recreationists:

- Equestrian and mountain bike trails are closed from November 15 (prior to traditional deer gun-hunting season) to May 1 (after the spring thaw).
- The trails are to be considered closed whenever conditions are too wet during the riding season. Over the years, riders have come to understand that an inch of rain or more and/or consecutive rain events make the trails too susceptible to damage, in addition to being a safety issue.
- Riding must stay on designated trails. With only a few exceptions, hikers, bicyclists, and equestrians share trails.
- Enforcement will be based on the honor system and by riders talking to other riders about the importance of protecting the trails for future use and not risk losing access altogether.

- Use fees are required per rider (or hiker, biker, skier), with funds being used to maintain the property.
- The KRMB made a commitment to building properly designed and sustainable trails that follow the contour of slopes, avoid sensitive species or sites, and minimize erosion.

During the public hearings on the proposed rules and the draft of the master plan held in La Farge, Ontario, and Madison, there was little input and few requests for changes, as many of the potentially confrontational topics like ATV use had already been settled. I had contacted representatives of the Sierra Club and Wisconsin Environmental Decade (since renamed Clean Wisconsin), as they had weighed in on the highway reconstruction, but neither organization commented on the specifics of the plan or rules. This lack of controversy provided a sense of relief that we had gotten it right.

Memorial Day Weekend in 2004 put the trail policies to the test. A full-time property manager with law enforcement credentials had been hired in March of that year. We also brought in a renowned Clemson University professor with expertise in trail planning and design to offer a workshop for the KVR staff and equestrian and mountain bike enthusiasts who were eager to volunteer. Work had begun on fixing or rerouting trails, and I applied for grant funding to install three timber bridges on the Old 131 Trail that would allow approximately five miles of access for all recreational users from the south end of the Reserve to Rockton.

Unfortunately, some horseback riders thought the process was going too slow and went back to using the closed routes. They ignored the wet conditions, and the horses left clear evidence of their violations throughout the Weister Creek and Black Hawk Rock quadrants. Following the incident, I drafted a letter on behalf of the board, with concurrence from the property manager, and mailed it to those who had registered as equestrians when they purchased their trail permit that holiday weekend, as well as to the equestrian organizations we'd come to know in the planning process. The letter reiterated the trail-use policy and threatened to take further action, including closing all trails, if violations continued. The board supported the staff and held their ground even though the riders were furious and contacted their elected officials, including the governor.

However, everyone backed the decision of the board to implement protective policies. This added credibility to the board's authority and set a precedent that damage to sensitive sites would not be tolerated. The combination of education, staff resources in property management, and enforcement was needed to demonstrate the overall management principles and rule implementation.

A group of recreationists who were impatient with the speed of trail work continued to press for more access and Band-Aid repairs. Mother Nature proved the need for sustainable construction during the back-to-back floods of 2007 and 2008. The only good thing that came out of the historic floods was an opportunity to show trail users that the KRMB was not opposed to riders but was opposed to repeatedly repairing trails susceptible to damage.

The floodwaters obliterated a major section of trail in the northern part of the Reserve. Instead of continuing the quick fixes of patching washouts only to have the same spot wash out again, the decision was made to close the damaged trail and redesign it sustainably for shared use by hikers, mountain bikers, and equestrian riders. Through grant funding and fee revenues, the KRMB contracted with a professional trail builder to the tune of $50,000 for the design and construction of a portion of that trail. The KVR staff completed the construction for the 3.5-mile section and, by following the design—which utilized the slope and contours to its advantage—demonstrated how a well-built, multiuse trail could save money, protect the property in the long run, and allow recreationists to see beautiful natural features along the way.

Eventually, multiuse became the policy for all repairs or reroutes throughout the sixty-plus miles of trails in the Reserve. Although tempers flared again between horseback riders and mountain bikers when they were forced to be on the same trails, the reality of potentially losing access overrode their displeasure at having to share trails. Educating visitors on trail etiquette through signage and on-site demonstrations also helped manage the people while protecting the property. Hikers and bicyclists yield to horses when they meet on the trails; it's simple and straightforward in the interest of safety because the horses are less likely to spook. In addition, horseback riders are advised not to bring a poorly trained horse to public property with frequent water crossings, a variety of wildlife, and the potential to meet other trail users. Challenges in shared trails still exist and will no doubt continue due to manure, ruts created by horse hooves, the speed of bikes startling other users, and the underlying bias of all users' preferences for their own hobbies.

Even though Wisconsin's Department of Natural Resources was not very popular with some residents who believed, rightly or wrongly, that the DNR was another Madison entity that would impose decisions on them, the department's ecologists, botanists, and conservation wardens were (and are still today) an invaluable resource for the KRMB to call on. To their credit, local and regional DNR staff participated in planning meetings, worked cooperatively on grant applications, and provided liaisons as needed for the early KRMB meetings. DNR ecologists and biologists served as tour guides to make sure the board members and I understood the significance of the unique habitats; provided inventory data on plants, birds, and water quality; and made recommendations for additional surveys.

Unlike DNR staff or other advisors, KRMB members have not necessarily been experts in natural resource management. Board members have been small business owners, artists, civil service retirees, or area residents who served on other local boards. A few of them were retired teachers with scientific backgrounds. The Ho-Chunk Nation representatives often wear two hats: as employees of the tribe's land management or cultural heritage departments and as board members for the Reserve. All board members share an interest in the management of this unique property. Grassroots input comes forward via subcommittees and through formal public input, which is an agenda item for each monthly meeting. Many of the board members attend events, instruct students, recreate on the land, or host groups that give firsthand feedback on how the KVR is doing.

In turn, they serve as a conduit to remind staff of community interests and involvement. One example is through unique aspects of the statutory language creating the KRMB, which has become more significant over the years. Specifically, Wisconsin State Statute 41.41(5) h states that the KRMB can "actively solicit bids for construction, materials, supplies, equipment and contractual services required by the board from bidders located in the region surrounding the Kickapoo valley reserve." The state of Wisconsin system normally requires agencies to purchase equipment or services like printing from a contract approved in Madison. The statutory authority to solicit bids and purchases from regional businesses has allowed the KRMB to become a valuable customer in this rural community, which helped to improve the government's relationship with residents and business owners.

In the five years prior to my departure, I witnessed all board members becoming more directly involved with the property, to everyone's benefit. Reggie Nelson, who grew up on the southern border of what is now the KVR and is the grandson of a former landowner, is an example of an active board member and a symbol of the next generation's influence on the future. As a mountain biker and kayaker who uses the Reserve, he politely reminds staff to keep the website current and offers photos and videos via his GoPro for use on the KVR's social media pages. He also sees firsthand the work of field staff and areas that may need some attention. More importantly, he interacts on-site with visitors, who are usually more than happy to share their opinions.

The evolution of this project gives both the board and staff great authority to manage the public land while at the same time offering flexibility to find a balance with the community and a wide variety of interests. The combination of residents' input through the policy-setting board, state government procedures as a statutorily recognized agency, co-management with the Ho-Chunk Nation, and input by interest groups on a variety of topics is an interesting administrative model that works well for this property.

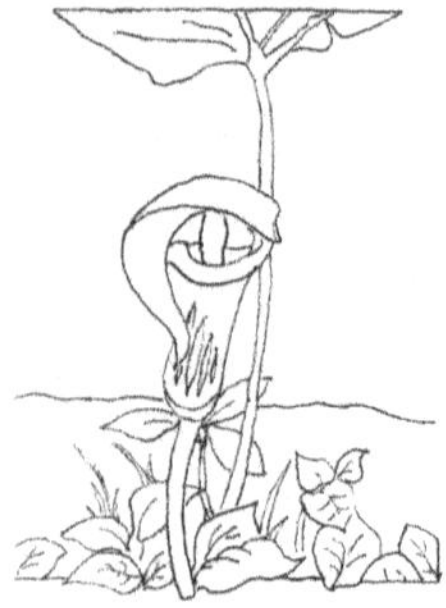

10 Riding the Riffles

Making a decent living in the Kickapoo Valley has always been difficult, and the La Farge Lake and Dam project had included efforts to attract tourists and their beneficial impact on the local economy. To address concerns about future economic development, the Citizen Advisory Committee's proposal for the Kickapoo Valley Reserve and future management plans also included goals to bring tourists to the valley.

Although the term *ecotourism* was in use by the mid-1980s, it took a while for this concept to be widely accepted. Dr. Rob Horwich of Community Conservation Inc. served on the Citizen Advisory Committee and had significant experience with biosphere protections in South America, although he lived in the Kickapoo Valley. Dr. Horwich referenced ecotourism in early versions of the proposal for the Reserve in 1991. He recognized that the area's scenic beauty, rural lifestyle, concentration of small organic farms, and the Amish community would be attractive to travelers and recreationists. Formal studies confirmed this tourism potential and noted that the right natural setting is a fundamental motivator for ecotourists.

Admittedly, I had little interest in or knowledge of economic development issues when I took the position of executive director. But I soon realized the Kickapoo Valley had the potential to attract outdoor enthusiasts, and tourists already impacted the project in terms of needing to protect it from them. The UW-Extension Tourism Research and Resource Center survey of 1993 verified that more than 12,000 people had canoed the river during that summer. During their visit, paddlers spent an estimated $655,000 (more than $1.4 million in 2024) for lodging, canoe rentals, groceries, and other items, according to John Leatherman's report on the survey in *At Work in the Kickapoo Valley*, published in 1994 through the University of Wisconsin Nuzum Fund grant.

The scenery in this region is naturally beautiful, and the KVR offers a variety of recreational and educational options for ecotourists who want to hike, ride horses or bikes, canoe, kayak, or go fishing. And the overriding mission to preserve and protect this diverse ecological gem fits the belief system of these tourists perfectly. They are more willing to support their favorite places financially through user and event fees when they know the funds help protect and maintain the property.

To illustrate the importance of the anticipated revenues for the local community from ecotourism, Governor Tommy Thompson directed the KRMB to be statutorily linked to the Wisconsin Department of Tourism for administrative support. This newly formed agency was charged with promoting all tourism in the state, would assist the KRMB with publications and event development, and serve as a liaison to area tourism businesses. Organizations such as the Kickapoo Valley Association, Vernon County Tourism, and Hidden Valleys were already promoting the area's unique scenery and recreation opportunities. Over the years, I attended or hosted countless tourism-related meetings and fundraisers that led to shared efforts on websites, brochure distribution through the visitor center, and the creation of special events. Cross-promotion of attractions and events had become part of my job even though the KVR practically promoted itself as word of mouth spread from visitors who fell in love with the place.

The board rejected requests for the KVR to include campgrounds with electrical hookups, showers, and other amenities, as they believed those types of facilities and other lodging options could be developed through private business. As a result, the twenty-three somewhat isolated campsites on the Reserve remain primitive—no potable water, toilets, or electricity—with a limit of ten people on most sites. In addition, campsites remained first-come, first-served for many years, so visitors could be more spontaneous or adjust their plans if weather conditions changed. This policy also eliminated competition with private campgrounds and the need for long-range planning for visitors who prefer to rough it.

In support of the increasing use of the Kickapoo River by canoeists and kayakers, access sites for paddlers were enhanced in conjunction with the highway reconstruction. A numbering system that had been in practice for many years labeled the bridge near the intersection of State Highways 33 and 131, at the southern end of the village of Ontario, as Bridge 1. However, the first bridge crossing the river is actually a few miles north of Ontario. During the planning process, I suggested the time was right to make the maps accurate by starting north of Ontario and eliminating the reference to Bridges 12 and 17, which had been removed during the planning of the lake and dam. The suggestion was not well received, to say the least. The canoe rental businesses strongly objected and convinced enough board members to keep the system as it was.

Most paddlers put in at Bridge 1 in the village of Ontario and float down to Bridge 4 or 5, and people camping at Wildcat Mountain State Park primarily use the park's landing, located upstream of Bridge 5. Although one shuttle service operates downstream out of Rockton, most of the existing shuttle services that provide canoes/kayaks, paddles, and life jackets to visitors are based in Ontario, north of the Reserve boundary. This popular stretch of river is easier for the shuttle services to maintain, clear logjams and access sites, and drop off and pick up their customers.

For many years, access was not managed. River enthusiasts had to be willing to slide down and climb up the riverbanks to get in and out of their canoes. Increased usage made popular sites susceptible to erosion as frequent use trampled vegetation and exposed the soil. Once the KRMB assumed management of the property, we designated river access sites in the management plans. Concrete ramps, gravel parking lots, and safe access to the highway were included in the DOT reconstruction plans, with funding through the WRDA and the state budget.

The popularity of canoeing in the area illustrates the need to find balance in the ecotourism equation. Over the years, the Kickapoo became known as a partiers' river. An easy, scenic float requiring minimal paddling skills gave rise to alcohol and drug use on summer weekends. Inebriated paddlers urinating in public, serious injuries, and disturbing amounts of litter on sandbars and access sites became problems. One of the shuttle services even hosted a special event in cooperation with a radio station in La Crosse that promised participants "all you can drink to and from La Crosse to Ontario for a day on the Kickapoo River."

But many paddlers came for the beauty and solitude, and a divide was widening between those who came to party and those who came to get away from it all. An editorial in the *Wisconsin State Journal* in 1999, reporting that canoe rental employees dumped the contents of canoes at Bridge 5 and stacked the boats like "slugs on the bank," brought this issue to a flash point. My love for the river definitely influenced my priorities on this matter. Canoe livery owners were invited to subcommittees and board meetings. Their businesses were becoming larger and more lucrative, but they faced little regulation or oversight. Wisconsin's constitutional reference to rivers being "common highways and forever free" was often cited as their authorization to continue to operate as they had for decades.

Eventually, an informal agreement came to pass. The KVR staff maintains five access sites within the Reserve, including gravel parking areas and porta-potties, during the busy summer season. After researching how litter and commercial-use issues were managed on other rivers, I brought a series of initiatives to the KRMB for formal approval. In 2014, we launched a campaign called Paddlers Pick Up that was modeled after a similar project in Iowa. Mesh bags were provided to paddlers through the shuttle services, Wildcat Mountain State Park, and the KVR, and paddlers were asked to pack their trash out and pick up other litter as they floated down the river. The bags are reusable, and the program was an amazing—and affordable—success. Extra efforts to encourage all visitors to pack out all their trash continue to expand, and litter is much less of an issue.

Glass containers and bottles are banned on the KVR portion of the river, and fines and citations can be issued to violators. Fees instituted at the parking areas help cover the costs for maintenance, and patrols have been added to protect the river and those who visit.

Logjams are a chronic problem on the river. Wind, high water, and unstable riverbanks send trees into the river that inevitably create a catchall for anything else coming down the river—including paddlers. Clearing logjams is dangerous, difficult work. Traditionally, the canoe liveries would cut their way through the jams and let the chunks float down to the next snag or bend. After discussions with a variety of other public properties that had to deal with similar issues, it became KVR's policy to drag as much of the debris out of the river as possible. A tractor or a professional logger with their heavy-duty logging skidder and winch are the best equipment to pull downed trees out of the floodplain so they don't end up back in the river during the next high-water event.

For many years, I went out with the field crew to clear logjams. I did this partly out of maternal instinct to try to protect the crew and make sure safety measures were followed, but it also gave me a good reason to get out of the office and on the river. I never had the strength to run the chainsaw—especially since maneuvering the snag required great balance while the weight of the tree and the pressure of the current created tremendous force—but I loved getting into the water to gather litter that the jam had collected or to pull branches out of the way. Our goal was simply to make the river passable, as it takes too much time and money to clear the biggest jams. When the final tree or branch was cut, and the space was big enough for canoes to pass through, there was always relief that our crew was safe and a sense of accomplishment knowing we'd also made it safer for others to enjoy this fabulous river.

Building the Visitor Center

The biannual budget introduced by Governor Tommy Thompson in 2000 included funding through the state's Knowles-Nelson Stewardship Fund for the construction of a visitor center at the KVR at an estimated cost of $2.3 million. It was an unusual funding source at the time, given that the Stewardship Fund was originally intended to purchase land, but I wasn't going to argue. Providing input on the design of the building was a high priority for the KRMB. Unfortunately, that was no easy task in the state system as Department of Administration officials were used to dealing with politicians and agency personnel but not with citizens who had survived a historic government boondoggle.

My first exposure to the state facilities process was when I was notified that the State Building Commission would be considering possible architects for the visitor center during one of their monthly meetings. For efficiency's sake, DOA staff selects the architects and makes recommendations to the commission on behalf of all state agencies. I drove the two hours to Madison, and as I settled into the back of the conference room for the subcommittee meeting, the six men at the table and the notetaker smiled politely. When the meeting started, they asked me to introduce myself, which I did.

"Why are you here?" they asked.

"Because we want to know who we'll be working with," I responded.

It was clear to me that they—with perfunctory approval of the commission—would decide who we'd work with. There was no opportunity for anyone else to provide background or voice an opinion. The meeting lasted approximately fifteen minutes, and the topic of the KVR Visitor Center took a total of thirty seconds. KEE Architecture had responded to the state's request for proposals, and the staff on the building commission who had worked with them on other projects assured me that they would be a good fit "for your little project."

We were fortunate the architect selected was willing to work with the board and staff to design a facility to reflect the beauty of the setting and the goals of the project. KRMB Chairman Ron Johnson frequently said that when people walked into the building, their first word should be "Wow!" Natural light, a color palette matching the surroundings, and a welcoming feel were stated goals for the building. One planning meeting even focused on the driveway and sidewalks. "Mother Nature designs nothing in a straight line," commented one board member. And so curved sidewalks lead visitors from the main parking area to the front door.

The Leadership in Energy and Environmental Design (LEED) certification was new to the private sector at the time and rather foreign to the DOA system. Although we requested it for consideration, it would have slowed the design and construction process. Several items on the KRMB's wish list were incorporated into the building to make it environmentally friendly even though it doesn't meet LEED standards; board members and I felt like each one was a bit of a win at the time. Here is what was used from our wish list:

- A bank of south-facing E-certified windows for passive solar heat, which make a huge difference during Wisconsin winters
- A deck that also serves as an outdoor classroom
- A geothermal heating and cooling system
- The use of timber harvested from the Reserve property
- Outdoor lighting shields that reduce light pollution and protect the dark sky for stargazing

The design also aimed for practicality wherever possible. Kid-friendly spaces require sinks in the classroom and indestructible concrete floors that are water-repellent and easy to clean. Direct access from indoor to outdoor spaces not only meets fire codes but also provides flexibility for instructors and students.

During the initial planning through to the final approval of the building's design and exhibit space, it was imperative that the story of the dam project and the people most directly impacted by it needed to be told. While other public buildings may have a list of those who donated money for the construction, a brick wall near the entryway to the KVR Visitor Center displays the 149 names of the families who were removed from the property via sale or eminent domain. When visitors ask if those names are from donors, the staff explains the people listed on the wall did not necessarily intend to be donors, which usually leads to more interest and questions that segue into the exhibits.

The interactive exhibits designed by the committee allowed for the space to feature four important themes:

- Geologic displays and information on the exceptional habitats in the Reserve
- Involvement of the Ho-Chunk Nation
- The history of flooding in the area and the abandoned dam and lake project
- The educational and recreational opportunities in today's Kickapoo Valley Reserve

Completed in 2004, the 8,300-square-foot visitor center contains a classroom, meeting room, exhibits, a library, a deck, and office space for staff. The visitor center hosts nearly 20,000 people annually for the general walk-through, as well as those who attend a mix of special events such as baby showers, class reunions, graduation parties, weddings, memorial services, and educational programs.

Education

The educational program provides year-round opportunities for students of all ages. Field trips in winter, spring, and fall allow schools to select from a curriculum that ranges from pond study to bird identification. Watching from my office window, I could see students on the deck learning the proper use of binoculars for birdwatching while other groups carried nets and buckets down to the pond. During the lunch break, the noise level grows exponentially as kids describe the *humongous* water boatmen they caught in the pond and others practice their barred owl calls: "*Who, who...who, whooooo.*"

Summer camps and weekend programs have also proven to be popular. The primary goal of these weeklong day camps is to get the students outside as much as possible. Topics vary from science-based to recreational adventures. The KVR is large enough for teenage campers to enroll in Wilderness Adventures, which involves carrying almost everything they need in their backpacks, hiking to backcountry sites, surviving without cell phones or video games for three days, cooking their own food, and connecting with a group of their peers. The Wilderness Adventure leaders utilize their training in antibullying, meditation, and nature immersion to guide the teens through these challenging excursions. In all our years of hosting these campers, we've never had a teen quit early or give a negative review. "Lifelong friendships" are often mentioned in the follow-up surveys. Nature-based education is now shown to be beneficial for a variety of learning styles, and the KVR is a unique site to put those styles into practice.

The long-standing education subcommittee and full-time education coordinator have done a great job of ensuring the education program attracts a variety of adults as well, with classes that focus on art, scavenging, and an assortment of guided hikes, such as for flower and bird identification and tours to the ice formations. The monthly guest-speaker series known as Driftless Dialogues, funded through the UW Foundation Nuzum grant, attracts a more regional audience on a variety of topics, and citizen monitoring projects for bats, frogs, and birds keep people engaged in lifelong learning. An ongoing astronomy program attracts stargazing hobbyists and experts alike, with the added bonus of promoting awareness of the need to protect the dark skies this rural region is well suited for.

Funding the KVR educational programs was always a significant challenge. The state of Wisconsin's appropriation for the KVR did not include additional funding specific to the programs. Fees, grants, special events, and donations support the education coordinator position, allow for the purchase of supplies and equipment, and pay for the instructors who teach under contract with the KVR. The Friends of the Kickapoo Valley Reserve is a vital asset for keeping the education program going and growing beyond original expectations.

Over the years, the property has also served as an exceptional site for a variety of research projects and on-site practicums for continuing education students and professors. Oak regeneration studies, begun through UW–Madison prior to the land ownership transfer, offer long-term opportunities to witness forestry changes. And ongoing bird surveys and plant inventories are valuable indicators of the health of the property.

For a real-life project experience, engineering students drafted the design for the KVR's timber bridges as part of a UW–Madison capstone course in 2003. The designs were invaluable for me when I worked with the U.S. Forest Service Forest Products Lab to construct the glulam timber Bridges 15, 16, and 18 that connect the Old 131 Trail. Coincidentally, the private consulting firm the KVR contracted with for the required ten-year inspection sent one of its current engineers to inspect a bridge he'd originally helped design when he was a student. He was thrilled to see the bridges had held up well, even after high-water events.

In addition, students from the University of Wisconsin in La Crosse and Baraboo come out for weekend recreation retreats to train for their future work as fitness instructors or teen mentors. Professors indicate the experiences are very popular and expose the undergraduates and graduates to a public property they were otherwise unfamiliar with.

KRMB members are often the ones to initiate weaving educational opportunities into projects whenever possible. One example is the five-year effort to restore Weister Creek, which flows from the western edge of the Reserve and feeds into the Kickapoo River just below Bridge 14. Since the creek is a decent trout stream, the COE, the DNR, and the Vernon County Land and Water Conservation Department installed lunker structures (wood or rock ledges) on the stream banks in the 1990s to provide cover for trout. The 2008 flood left significant snags, debris, and washouts. Some of the banks collapsed, and others were choked with mud. Led by KRMB member Paul Hayes, the post-flood restoration was planned as a habitat restoration project rather than a species-specific trout stream project.

An extensive consortium was brought together, including Trout Unlimited, the Vernon County Conservation Department, Ho-Chunk Nation staff, the UW–Madison, and DNR fish biologists, botanists, herpetologists, ornithologists, and engineers. The result is a three-mile stream corridor with properly shaped banks to diffuse the energy of the floodwater. It includes prairie plantings, turtle hibernacula, intentionally constructed backwater pools for amphibians, a sand pile for nesting swallows, and carefully submerged logs that create deep plunge pools for the cold, oxygen-rich water that the native trout need to thrive.

Planned and completed in five phases from 2014 to 2019, the project is serving as an educational model for habitat restoration. The finished phases withstood the historic 2017 and 2018 floods, while the unrestored segments showed how badly floodwater could damage the banks. Water quality testing and bird, frog, fish, and plant surveys will continue to teach us what went right and what could be done differently on other sites. A variety of groups have toured the project, and multiple media articles have featured the collaboration and innovative approach. The technical standards are now widely used by federal and state agencies and by Trout Unlimited and other groups dedicated to restoring habitats and improving stream quality.

Place Attachment

Graduates of natural resource management programs quickly learn their job isn't to manage property; it's to manage people. This lesson has been on full display at the KVR as policies were established and programs expanded. In addition to Native Americans' and the former landowners' attachments to the land, the property has attracted a varied fan base that supports it and is also crucial to its long-term protection.

Thousands of people are now attached to this place. Significant milestones are celebrated here, such as marriage proposals, weddings, outdoor classes, catching a personal best trout, or completing one's first triathlon. Understanding how these relationships might affect residents' or tourists' behavior in the future would be an interesting area of research. I assume they would feel even more protective, although they may also have a sense of ownership that clouds their willingness to share the space with others.

Local perception in the Kickapoo Valley seems to be split. Some multigenerational families residing in the valley are not confident that tourism is economically beneficial to the area, as they see recreationists hauling in goods purchased elsewhere while paying only $15 a night to camp. Stagnating student enrollment and the resulting difficulty in funding local schools are also indicators that everyday life is not improving for all rural residents. Blaming the failed dam project and the KVR for the valley's current problems is, for some people, a hard habit to break, and having to deal with rules about what they can and cannot do on the government land also frustrates those who remember being able to do anything they wanted on what was considered a no-man's-land.

However, many newcomers to the valley cite the quality of life, the landscape, and features like the Reserve as reasons for their moving here. A case in point is the evolution of Viroqua, a town of roughly 4,500 people located fifteen miles west of the KVR. In the past fifteen years, businesses such as the Driftless Café (a pioneering farm-to-table restaurant), the Driftless Angler (which provides trout fishing guides and supplies), Bluedog Cycles, Wonderstate Coffee, and the Viroqua Food Cooperative have been established and provide what eco-conscious young families and tourists find attractive. A Waldorf school, a thriving farmers market, live music venues and festivals, a community radio station, and increased employment opportunities at nearby Organic Valley Cooperative contribute to the unique place the Vernon County seat of Viroqua has become.

In 2019, 28 percent of the total annual KVR permits sold were in the Viroqua zip code, and these newcomers are an important source of financial and political support for the Reserve. Increased donations and participation in fundraising events, education programming, and volunteer projects are vital to the success of the programs.

Demonstrating to longtime residents and newcomers that the Reserve provides opportunities for both residents and tourists will continue to be a challenge. Examining the demographics of local children and grandchildren who move away for college and careers, only to return as residents or repeat tourists, could also be the subject of a future survey or research project. The KVR staff already provides one small study group. In 2021, four of the five permanent staff were born and raised in the region, went to college, and held other jobs, then returned to the valley in their thirties to work on this unique project. Five out of the seven part-time employees were from multigenerational families in the valley.

Whether through a fond memory or dedicated work as an employee, people's attachment to the property and project has evolved considerably. Managing the benefits for these rural communities while protecting the river and its surrounding landscape will take valiant efforts for generations to come.

11
Reflections

Thinking recently about the twenty-four years since the Kickapoo Valley Reserve was officially formed, I allowed myself to indulge in some *what-ifs*:

> **What if the dam had never been proposed?** Residents frustrated with the repeated flooding would have relocated; others would have continued to live at the mercy of the devastating high-water events that have now proven to be more frequent and intense.
>
> **What if the dam had been completed?** This scenario is easier to imagine, as we can look at other examples of projects like this, such as Lake Wisconsin, located eighty miles east of the Kickapoo Valley. The dam on the Wisconsin River that created this lake is bigger than what was planned for the Kickapoo, and it has the added purpose of generating electricity. It did bring more recreational possibilities and development opportunities to that area. However, this manipulated body of water still experiences flooding and poor water quality, and some residents invest thousands of dollars annually to dredge the silt from their lakefront property due to sedimentation from runoff.

The Kickapoo watershed is a smaller system, but the long-term problems were similar. According to the UW study done in 1974, if the upstream communities and landowners had not improved wastewater treatment plants and septic systems and implemented strict conservation standards for farm fields, Lake La Farge would have been a shallow, eutrophic, and unhealthy system. Unfortunately, there have *not* been enough improvements to the systems upstream. Sedimentation and nutrient loading continue to be significant issues impacting water quality throughout the watershed.

What if the land had been sold to the highest bidder after construction stopped? Some forms of development would have probably occurred, perhaps a golf course, condominiums, or private campgrounds, which were all suggested in the early planning phase. The resulting increase in taxes may have helped rural communities. However, the local units of government would also have had to consider the cost of the infrastructure needed for developments, such as roads and bridges, which often outpaces the increase in tax revenue. Not to mention, any development would have had to plan for or recover from frequent flooding and offered little protection for the resource.

What if the land had been transferred to the National Park Service or the Bureau of Indian Affairs? Either of those entities would have presumably protected the property, but residents' ability to have input on policy decisions would have been minimal. The aids in lieu of tax payments would not have been nearly as lucrative to the local municipalities, and the visitor fees would have been pooled for national redistribution, not returned specifically to this property.

It is interesting to note a point from former extension agent Al Anderson, who said, "Had the project started two years earlier, the Kickapoo River would have been dammed to create Lake La Farge;

had it started two years later, there wouldn't have been a shovel of dirt moved." While ruminating on the what-ifs can be futile and changing a tumultuous history is impossible, learning from the story is valuable.

Environmental Lessons

The 8,600-acre KVR is the "best example of ecological diversity in the entire Driftless Region," according to Eric Epstein, a retired biologist with the Wisconsin DNR. What is it that makes it the best? Learning the significance of what is here should further justify protection.

Land Cover

A bird's-eye view of the Reserve reveals the dominance of woodland. Sixty percent of the land is forested with mixed hardwoods and conifer. Seventeen percent is covered with water and wetlands, mainly in the valley bottoms. Approximately 12 percent, or 700 acres, is leased agricultural land that is primarily used to grow corn and soybeans. The remaining open lands are a mix of former pasture, grasslands, prairie, or native grass establishment—restoration efforts that began nearly thirty years ago.

Wetlands

On the valley floor, the Kickapoo River floodplain features a mosaic of wetland habitats. Sedge meadow and marsh habitats characterize river meanders and old river oxbows. Springs and seeps feed isolated wetlands and ephemeral ponds. Ecologists prize the wooded wetlands, also referred to as swamps, that are dominated by shrubs and trees. These areas may only have a few inches of surface water in the spring, but the timing is crucial to frogs, insects, and nesting birds.

Previous human impact created depressions that evolved into wetlands. As drain tiles were no longer maintained adjacent to agriculture fields, wetland systems throughout the Reserve rebounded. Unfortunately, past agricultural practices also introduced the aggressive and invasive reed canary grass that grows so dense that it does not allow as many acres to reach their full potential as diverse, productive habitats. The silt loam soils are crucial to holding moisture year-round, especially during the flood events that happen throughout the valley. As rain events are forced through this narrow valley, the wetland areas now function as a buffer to slow and hold some of the floodwaters.

Flora

Inventories list 403 plant species within the Reserve, 322 of which are native. Sixteen rare or threatened species have been documented. Rare flora found on the Reserve include cliff cudweed (*Pseudognaphalium saxicola*), rock clubmoss (*Lycopodium porophyllum*), purple-stem cliff brake (*Pellaea atropurpurea*), hooker orchid (*Platanthera hookeri*), bird's-eye primrose (*Primula mistassinica*), and lance-leaved buckthorn (*Rhamnus lanceolata*).

Non-native species are recognized as a serious threat to the integrity of the landscape as they can spread rapidly and interfere with, dominate, or replace native plant communities.

To date, the most aggressive invasive species found on the Reserve and those of major concern are garlic mustard (*Alliaria petiolata*), honeysuckle (*Lonicera*), glossy buckthorn (*Rhamnus frangula*), black locust (*Robinia pseudoacacia*), multiflora rose (*Rosa multiflora*), spotted knapweed (*Centaurea maculosa*), leafy spurge (*Euphorbia esula*), purple loosestrife (*Lythrum salicaria*), yellow and white sweet clovers (*Melilotus officinalis*), wild parsnip (*Pastinaca sativa*), and reed canary grass (*Phalaris arundinacea*).

Because of the many farms and homes that were once located on the Reserve, non-native flora associated with former residents' gardens and landscaping remains on the property. Exotics such as lilacs, tulips, and peonies can be seen blooming among native species.

Fauna

Wildlife on the Reserve includes a variety of mammal, bird, reptile, and amphibian species. The significant size of the Reserve and its bountiful combination of forest, grassland, agriculture fields, and water, in conjunction with minimized human impact, make it an idyllic habitat for an assortment of species, including those common to the Midwest, such as white-tailed deer, gray squirrel, coyote, and raccoon.

Rare animal species known to inhabit the property include three species threatened in Wisconsin: the Cooper's hawk (*Accipiter cooperii*), the red-shouldered hawk (*Buteo lineatus*), and the wood turtle (*Glyptemys insculpta*). Other animals of special concern include Kentucky warblers (*Oporornis formosus*), worm-eating warblers (*Helmitheros vermivorum*), cerulean warblers (*Dendroica cerulea*), and cherrystone drops (*Hendersonia occulta*), which are globally rare snails found on cool, moist, rocky slopes.

Forest Freaks

Former and current foresters' and botanists' inventories enthusiastically praise the forested land within the Reserve. From a cultural sense, evidence can still be found of oak-dominant habitats west of the Kickapoo River that experienced fire prior to European influences of logging, crop farming, and grazing. Closed canopy woodlands east of the river, consisting of sugar maple, basswood, oak, hickory, and white pine, are likewise indicative of a unique landscape, as referenced by settlers' stories telling of the challenges to settle the area.

More notable is when the descriptive generalizations are abandoned for a more specific imagery of what is seen within the forests. River or yellow birch and hemlock are common in the Reserve along the river corridor and tributaries. Historically and currently, each documented inventory will note these are species that are more suited to northern Wisconsin. Still, they thrive within the Kickapoo watershed. The impressive size and age of some of the remnant white pine and oak are also frequently highlighted since they may have only survived because the terrain was too difficult to harvest trees on. For example, a large wood cookie displayed in the visitor center exhibits is from a white oak that fell during a storm in 2014 and was determined to be more than 200 years old.

Perhaps the biggest source of support for the magnificent mix of flora and fauna is that the property is so large. Contiguous blocks of forests, such as the Bridge 8 Woods within the Reserve, at more than 1,000 acres, would be considered small in most national parks west of the Mississippi. However, for southwest Wisconsin and the Driftless Region, the woods are important for a variety of species, as the DNR's Eric Epstein noted:

> Encompassing significant environmental gradients of soil moisture, slope, aspect, and composition, Bridge

> 8 supports many native plant and animal species that persist and thrive in such habitats and which may be scarce in or absent from the vast majority of the smaller, more fragmented, often isolated, and sometimes highly disturbed forest remnants so prevalent across much of southern Wisconsin.[11]

Publicly protected lands are relatively scarce in the Driftless Region. If we add the adjoining acreage of Wildcat Mountain State Park, at roughly 3,500 acres, with the 8,600 acres in the Reserve, plus ever-increasing protected acres through private landowners choosing to put their land in conservation easements or donations to land conservancies, the habitats and diverse mix of plants and animals they support are vitally important.

Ecosystems, by definition, are a variety of components coming together to provide a network of interdependence and co-exist as a system. From the natural geologic history to the diversity of the flora and fauna that exists on the Reserve, it is clearly the sum of its parts that combine to create a landscape-scale ecosystem worthy of the level of public protection it has achieved. The microclimates that begin with cold water percolating through layers of rock to support invertebrates and small plants, which then support insects and vascular plants, including eighty-foot-tall hemlock relics and 200-year-old white pines, are what create this unique place. To have 8,600 acres of publicly protected property with large contiguous blocks of forest and amazingly diverse plant species adjacent to an ancient free-flowing river makes the Reserve an ecological marvel worthy of the highest levels of protection.

Administrative Lessons

Environmental protection has evolved to a point where structure is needed to ensure that the public, businesses, and governmental agencies do the right thing. Although we first relied heavily on the honor system for everything from purchasing permits to people cleaning up after themselves, we soon realized that members of the public are accustomed to looking for direction in public spaces.

11 Description utilized within the original Kickapoo Valley Reserve Master Plan to justify the Natural Areas designation for portions of the Reserve. Print document archived at the KVR Visitor Center library collection.

Now more than ever, I believe enforcing administrative rules and implementing management plans are crucial to protecting unique habitats.

The KRMB's mix of personalities, experiences, and skills have come together to successfully manage this diverse public property. One main drawback to the administrative structure is the link to politics. Over the years, some board positions have been left vacant by delays in the governor's appointments even though qualified candidates had applied. Clearly the KRMB is a small entity in the vast network of state government, but completing appointments in a timely manner is critical to having a functional board with new energy and ideas. It is hoped these delays are not the first signs of partisanship creeping into a historically bipartisan project.

Also challenging for the KRMB is its reliance on larger state agencies for accounting, information technology, payroll, and human resources. Adapting to this bureaucratic structure continues to be a work in progress for the KRMB and KVR employees. For example, following bidding rules or having to consider liability concerns sometimes delays repair work after flood events. The checks and balances of government systems are needed to verify the use of public dollars but are not designed for speedy recovery in times of need. On the positive side, the requirement of financial reporting to both the KRMB and the Wisconsin Department of Administration provides transparency to ensure the public that the funds are used properly and projects are done right.

The base funding allocation through the state of Wisconsin provides the operating budget for the Reserve. Specifically designated from the Conservation Fund within the state accounts, it supports the maintenance and operations of the visitor center, four full-time permanent employees, and the payment in lieu of taxes to local municipalities and schools. When this administrative structure causes frustration, alternatives such as becoming a nonprofit or operating through a land trust are quickly dismissed in recognition of the vital funding appropriated on behalf of all Wisconsin taxpayers. When I started in 1996, the total budget was just under $190,000; fast-forward to the annual report for fiscal year 2022 with a reported $550,000 base allocation and a total for the overall operating budget—base allocation and revenue—at slightly more than $1 million!

Most notable is the foresight of those who drafted the legislation for the KRMB to allow revenues generated from the Reserve to fund maintenance of the property and the education programs. Revenue from leased agriculture fields and timber harvests has provided desperately needed funds for sustainable trail reconstruction and habitat restoration. Fees for trail use, camping, parking, and special events generate enough revenue to cover costs for mowing, porta-potties at river access sites, gravel replacement after floods, and the part-time staff who do ongoing maintenance work. The education programs also charge user fees. However, keeping costs affordable for schools and families while still paying instructors and purchasing supplies is a constant challenge.

Last but not least is the incredible support received through the nonprofit, volunteer-based Friends of the Kickapoo Valley Reserve, which was officially formed in 2000 by a core group of residents. Brad Steinmetz, a lifelong resident and retired history teacher, and Orville Jensen, then the manager of Nuzum's lumberyard in La Farge, began discussing the idea with me. In quick succession, a local attorney drafted the application to the IRS for 501(c)(3) nonprofit status, and a Friends board was formed with a list of ideas.

The first project the Friends tackled was installing a cover over a bridge. Even though Bridge 18, a glulam timber bridge on the south end of the property, was already in place, KRMB member George Nettum was pushing for a covered bridge to impress people as they entered the main trail through the Reserve. The Department of Administration's Division of Facilities Development said taxpayer dollars could not be spent on "decorations." The Friends of the Kickapoo Valley Reserve raised money, received an impressive discount on supplies, and had some guys they happened to know from a construction company put a roof on Bridge 18. It is a beautiful legacy to George Nettum and shows the tenacity of the Friends group, who have been an integral part of the success of the Reserve ever since.

Communication and coordination have been the key to ensuring the Friends board of directors is in sync with the mission and goals of the Reserve. The president of the Friends of the KVR has always been invited to the monthly KRMB meetings, and KVR staff members attend the Friends board meetings. Since the inception of the Friends group, volunteers have donated countless hours for events and special projects. More than $500,000 has been raised to support the education programs and projects at the Reserve. In an era when funding through the state of Wisconsin has not kept up with need, the Friends group continues to grow in membership, and its fundraising makes up for a significant part of this shortfall.

Rural Economics

Various studies have indicated that public properties can be an economic benefit to adjacent communities. A 2023 report from Headwaters Economics showed that visitors to Glacier National Park in rural Montana generated roughly $185 million in revenue for local communities.[12] Granted, the KVR is not the size of Glacier National Park, but anecdotal evidence shows the KVR is having a positive effect on the economy of neighboring communities and local businesses.

Area realtors report homes and land bordering the Reserve sell rapidly and the selling prices are higher on average than other acreage in the area. Early in my tenure, I had the opportunity to meet Phil Lewis, then a professor of landscape architecture and director of the Environmental Awareness Center at the University of Wisconsin–Madison. The center was a map nerd's dream, with floor-to-ceiling diagrams of the regions he was studying. Professor Lewis understood the importance of the Driftless Area as the "doughnut hole" in the circular city concept. The millions of people who reside in urban areas like Milwaukee, Chicago, and Minneapolis/St. Paul would seek out opportunities in the Driftless core, which was only a few hours' drive for them.

Since 2000, more than twenty new homes or cabins have been constructed on the perimeter of the Reserve. Two of those structures struck me as particularly interesting because the owners' families had supported the completion of the dam and had invested time and money in hopes of land development around the lake. Although one family was more bitter than the other, both families' adult children inherited the land and built their own homes with a beautiful view overlooking the Reserve. Each told me how much they love the

---

12 Flyr M, and L. Koontz. 2023. 2022 national park visitor spending effects: Economic contributions to local communities, states, and the nation. Natural Resource Report NPS/NRSS/EQD/NRR—2023/2551. National Park Service, Fort Collins, Colorado, https://doi.org/10.36967/2299764.

security of knowing they'll never have neighbors blocking the view.

Prices for recreational land have ups and downs in line with financial markets, but the parcels adjacent to the KVR have steadily increased in price. There are exceptions, of course, but the speed of sale and per-acre prices are noteworthy for this region. In 2019, a 335-acre parcel adjoining the Reserve came up for sale with a list price of roughly $2 million. Board members and I were interested in protecting it, as it included the only remaining privately owned segment of the Kickapoo River that's within the KVR, and it is home to one of the healthiest populations of the northern monkshood plant and other wonderful natural features. In cooperation with the Mississippi Valley Conservancy, we commissioned an appraisal. The appraised value was $1.3 million, but shortly after receiving the report, we learned a man from Chicago had paid full price for the land. We can only hope he is interested in protecting it too.

The evolution of the KVR corresponds to another major development in the Kickapoo Valley. Organic Valley Cooperative started in 1988 with a few farmers and the idea that food could be produced at a fair price for the farmer and without the use of chemical herbicides, pesticides, or synthetic fertilizers. Headquartered in La Farge, Organic Valley has grown to employ more than 900 people and reports approximately 1,500 farms as members of the cooperative nationwide according to their website.[13] Products are sold nationally and internationally and the La Farge headquarters overlooks the Kickapoo Valley Reserve. Organic Valley's ongoing commitment to rural small towns is impressive, and its presence in the area has led to a major increase in employment opportunities for people attracted to the rural lifestyle and the recreational possibilities provided by the Reserve and the river.

Evidence that the KVR attracts recreation dollars also exists. A research project funded through the UW Foundation Nuzum Fund calculated trout fishing anglers brought $1.1 million into the area in 1999. The results for canoeing were equally significant, with an estimated 16,000 paddlers bringing $1.2 million in new spending and supporting forty-five local jobs in the Kickapoo Valley area during 1999. The same study noted a shortage of lodging options for

---

13 Organic Valley annual report, 2021, https://www.organicvalley.coop/why-organic-valley/sustainability/impact-report/.

recreationists and a lack of other activities beyond canoeing on the Kickapoo River.[14] Since that time, a variety of new rental cabins, bed and breakfasts, motels, and hotels within twenty miles of the Reserve have alleviated this shortage to some extent.

The addition of biking, hiking, and special events has provided options for additional recreation. Music events, specialty shops, Amish-made goods, and new restaurants have also broadened the choices for tourists visiting the area. Two additional canoe livery/shuttle services have opened in the past decade, which brings the total number of canoes and kayaks available to rent on this section of the river to more than 1,000 boats and tubes.

The annual Dam Challenge Triathlon (canoe/kayak, bike, and run) attracts nearly 500 participants on the first Saturday in October each year. In 2016, at a KRMB meeting, the Wisconsin Economic Development Corporation calculated the event brought in more than $100,000 in increased tourist revenue over the weekend. It is also a critical fundraiser for the education program, with additional revenue from sponsorships, registration fees, and the ever-popular pasta supper hosted by the Friends of the KVR.

Wisconsin's legendary winter season poses certain challenges when it comes to economic development via ecotourism. Early trout fishing and turkey hunting seasons bring visitors in the spring, while people who come to view fall colors and hunt deer and pheasants bring tourist dollars through November, but December through March is considered the slow season for tourism-related businesses. A lack of consistent snow cover limits the options for snowmobiling, cross-country skiing, and snowshoeing, but unique events like guided hikes to ice formations—where seeps in the sandstone outcrops create magnificent icicles—have drawn visitors from throughout the Midwest during the winter. On one Saturday in February 2018, more than 200 people hiked in the Reserve on a sunny but chilly eighteen-degree day. Although many of these hikers were local, permit records showed zip codes from Chicago, Minneapolis, Madison, and Milwaukee. Special events like the Winter Festival in January and the art programs in March also give tourists who love the Reserve a reason to come back in the off-season.

---

14 Canoeing and Angling in Southwest Wisconsin, report summary by Al Anderson, Laura Hewitt, and Dave Marcouillier, 2001 https://dpla.wisc.edu/wp-content/uploads/sites/1021/2017/06/01canoeanglefactsheet.pdf.

The Most Important Question

When considering the history and future goals of the KVR, we (collectively) must continue to ask this important question: Have we gotten it right in terms of preserving cultural history and protecting the ecological diversity on the property?

The story of the failed dam project is often told without much attention to Native American history. It is my hope that all future education programs, events, and exhibit upgrades will bring a better balance to the story of the Reserve. While the establishment of the Upper Kickapoo Valley Prehistoric Archeological District and the federal and state laws protecting the remaining sites are significant, they may give a false sense of confidence that the artifacts and sacred sites are completely protected, as KRMB member and Ho-Chunk Nation Tribal Historic Preservation Officer Bill Quackenbush pointed out. When I asked if we were doing enough, he responded via email:

> Current KVR management practices do not incorporate preservation steps within their day-to-day activities other than the inclusion of a component of a cultural review during proposed projects that include soil-disturbance activities. Although considered during a proposed project, there are no status updates on sites known within the Reserve at the state level. Site visits are not documented unless there's been a disturbance to them, nor are there any known plans to update the records of these sites on the WHS Archeological Sites Inventory to ensure the sites have been properly protected against adverse effects since the establishment of the Reserve. Regarding proposed projects where archeological sites are considered—trail work, forestry practices, agriculture lease sites, and ongoing maintenance/management work—avoidance of immediate sites does not constitute a definitive cultural resource management plan.

Bill is right, of course. There has not been a status update of the known sites since the inventory of 1997–98 in preparation for the MOU. Hiring qualified staff to do further updates seems out of reach after years of budget cuts, and archeological study requires layers of certification that most of the KVR staff simply don't have. The State

Historic Preservation Office and the Mississippi Valley Archeology Center based at the University of Wisconsin–La Crosse are currently the best assets to keep proposed projects from damaging sites. Ideally, someone from the UW system or the Ho-Chunk Nation will host an instructional course or bring archeology students to the Reserve to check on the known sites, similar to how we update bird, forest, and plant inventories at regular intervals.

Successful environmental protection is hard to gauge. We are fortunate to have collected records of the numerous inventories and studies done on the Reserve. These reports give current and future managers an important understanding of what was here and what the property can support in terms of flora and fauna. If we consider only what was here prior to the establishment of the Reserve—conventional farm and pastureland, little or no water protection or septic system rules—and what it could have been—a dammed river with a stagnant water body (assuming sewer, septic, and agriculture rules remained unchanged)—then, yes, the natural environment is better protected now. Comparing it to its pre-settlement condition, it would probably not fare so well.

It is unfortunate that the diverse bird and plant species found on the Reserve can't speak for themselves, as balancing recreation and revenue generation puts them at risk. Horse hooves and logging equipment can bring in invasive plant species. The serenity of the large contiguous block of Bridge 8 Woods is interrupted every Saturday from May through October by thousands of people floating down the river. Wisconsin's white-tailed deer population has exploded, and the number of hunters has gone down, making forest regeneration efforts futile. Eventually, the scale may tip toward more recreation and amenities if more tourist dollars are desired. The KRMB members, in cooperation with the Ho-Chunk Nation, the Friends of KVR, and neighboring communities and businesses, will need to decide whether preservation is more important than enhanced recreation.

The history, mission, and goals of the Reserve need to be revisited on a regular basis by the board members, the Ho-Chunk Nation, KVR staff, the Friends of KVR, and the public to refresh the commitment to preserve and protect the property. When new projects, events, or policy decisions are considered, there needs to be a thorough understanding of what the long-term impact could be and how protective measures to prevent those potential problems are addressed. Former Chairman Ron Johnson and I would often use the phrase "quality over quantity." Bigger, more, and new aren't always the best for this old river system. At some point, the impact of the increasing number of visitors will have to be balanced with the benefits of their visit.

12

Beware of Sweeps and Strainers

Change brought about through outside forces is constant, and so is the need for vigilance. I am sharing the following story to illustrate how important this is for protecting both the natural landscape and the unique management structure of the Kickapoo Valley Reserve.

It was a typical Wednesday night in February 2015 at the KVR Visitor Center. The night's featured speaker in the Driftless Dialogue lecture series was just wrapping up, and the thirty-five people in attendance were ready to call it a night. The series is sponsored through the University of Wisconsin Foundation's Nuzum Fund and administered through the UW–Madison's College of Agriculture and Life Sciences. While an entire chapter could be devoted to this man, for this part of the story, it's enough to know that Ralph Nuzum made a bequest to the UW Foundation in the mid-1970s to connect the UW system with the Kickapoo Valley. By bringing professors, scientists, and other experts to research and speak on a variety of topics related to the region, Ralph Nuzum's bequest is a success by any measure and a great example of the "Wisconsin Idea" in action—a long-standing tenet that education should influence people's lives beyond the classroom statewide.

Surprisingly, that evening, I received a text message from a legislative staffer alerting me that then-Governor Scott Walker's budget proposal had just been released and included a proposal to transfer the Kickapoo Reserve Management Board to the Department of Natural Resources. *What the?* We had no knowledge that this was being discussed, much less formally proposed. This move might have made sense on paper to many because, in some ways, the Reserve looks like a state park. However, the history and current management are nothing like a state park, so this would be a huge shift for a project that had been progressing nicely since 1997.

The Ho-Chunk Nation leadership was livid that the Walker administration had not recognized that the proposal would directly impact trust lands within the Reserve and that the tribe, therefore, deserved consultation as a sovereign nation. But who put the proposal into the budget, and why doesn't matter. It turned out that the proposal was purely a policy initiative, not a cost-saving measure, as the funding and number of employees would remain the same. And the KRMB wasn't the only one targeted; the Lower Wisconsin State Riverway Board was facing the same challenge. As word spread of the proposed transfer to the DNR, people from near and far began asking what could be done to prevent it.

To understand why this proposal was such a big deal, it's important to remember the history of residents' dealings with the government in general and especially Wisconsin's Department of Natural Resources. Many lifelong residents believe to this day that the DNR was responsible for the 1975 decision to stop the construction of the dam. For people who supported damming the Kickapoo River and creating a man-made lake in the early 1970s, their version of the DNR acronym was more likely to be "Damn Near Russia." Meanwhile, residents who had moved here since the mid-1970s quickly came to share the concern that management decisions for this expansive piece of land in their shared backyard might be made somewhere far away from the valley.

The proposal also came on the heels of a series of sweeping changes made by Governor Walker that caused a bit of whiplash no matter which political party you were aligned with. From dramatic changes for public school teachers to right-to-work legislation, Wisconsin's political climate was no longer conducive to grassroots input or bipartisan initiatives. Valley residents had seen politics rule over reason before and didn't want to go through it again.

United at Last

Wisconsin's budget process requires the governor—in conjunction with state agencies—to propose a two-year budget to the legislature's Joint Committee on Finance, which works through the details and sends a budget to the state legislature for approval. The governor's proposal came out in February, and the legislature indicated the budget would be finalized by the end of June, in time for the start of the new fiscal year on July 1, 2015. We had our deadline.

Concerns were expressed to KRMB members and me about the KVR being absorbed into the DNR. As the second-largest state agency with extensive program and enforcement responsibilities to protect the environment statewide, the DNR was already responsible for more than its ever-shrinking staff could manage. Outlandish rumors circulated that the Walker administration had requested the transfer so the land could be sold to China. More credible were the emails and phone calls asking if the KRMB would retain policy-making authority over how the 8,600 acres were to be managed. Another concern was whether staff would retain their jobs or whether the DNR would assign staff based on its reorganization plan.

The KRMB invited the district's legislators, State Senator Jennifer Shilling (D) and State Representative Lee Nerison (R), to a public meeting. The room overflowed with concerned citizens and people representing a variety of organizations. Lifelong residents who had once supported the proposal for a man-made lake spoke on behalf of keeping the Reserve as a citizen-managed property. Even though horseback riders and mountain bikers hadn't often seen eye to eye, they agreed that the property needed to retain autonomy. This time, the people came to the defense of the Reserve as a united front. Senator Shilling and Representative Nerison promised to inform their respective party leaders that this item in the governor's budget proposal should be deleted.

Fans of the Reserve took the lead in contacting legislators throughout the state, and the governor's staff indicated they were hearing directly from constituents too. Appointed board members and state employees are restricted from lobbying elected officials in Wisconsin. Even though political activity is limited, the KRMB members and staff were allowed to identify topics of concern about this proposed change. It is also a risk to oppose a governor's recommendation, given you may need them to consider future budget or program requests. Since it wasn't clear if the Departments of Natural Resources and Tourism had requested the change, it would look strange to oppose them as well.

But it was fortunate that the Ho-Chunk Nation was under no such restraint. Along with other ongoing issues they had with the state government, their president and legislative liaisons made the proposal to transfer the Reserve to the DNR a talking point during meetings with various state officials. Their opposition was clearly communicated, and it obviously had an impact.

The Joint Committee on Finance unanimously supported the resolutions drafted by Senator Shilling and Representative Nerison to reject the administration's transfer proposal. In addition, the Legislative Fiscal Bureau staff was aware of the problems the KRMB had had with the requirement that budget and staffing requests go through the Department of Tourism secretary. The resolution included wording for the KRMB to be assigned its own agency number, which ensured even more autonomy for future budgets. In the end, the local citizens, user groups, and the Ho-Chunk Nation, who all shared the belief this unique project was worth fighting for, prevailed.

The Need for Constant Attention

Prior to this crisis, I had felt like my work for the Reserve was close to completion. Ownership had been transferred, policies had been implemented and enforced, and two decades of shared management had proven that the Ho-Chunk Nation and residents could work together to take care of the largest public property in southwest Wisconsin and make it a success. The knot had been untangled, the boondoggle was only a history lesson, and the river would be protected for eternity.

But it is not.

The near miss with a governor's directive in 2015 illustrates the need for ongoing vigilance in protecting this river and property. Laws, policies, and directives change frequently in this country, and the Reserve shouldn't rest on its laurels.

Pressure is constant from the staff, board members, user groups, and the public to make the land and river do more—more trails, more access, larger campsites with more amenities, more special events, and other impacts in remote areas. It has been a slippery slope where one small, approved change becomes the justification for the next one.

On any given summer Saturday, a paddler hoping to enjoy the beauty of the Kickapoo River will be joined by hundreds of other canoers and kayakers who may be more interested in how much beer they can drink than the number of cedar waxwings they see along the way. The Reserve is not the first public property to be at risk of being "loved to death."

The KRMB and the Reserve staff also deal regularly with diametrically opposed situations. For example, the same instructor who requests a closed-door meeting with me to discuss his concerns over the use of herbicides on invasive plant species will also request permission to allow thirty-plus people to camp at a backcountry site for a retreat he's guiding. Again, we're not managing the resource; we're managing *people's impact* on the resource.

The KRMB's monthly meetings spend more time on attempts to expand recreation than on preserving and protecting the Reserve. Controlling invasive species, habitat restoration, and improving water quality should be a priority set by the board and carried out by staff. Rather than implying that it's an administrative hassle or delay, the archeological and environmental surveys should be viewed by the staff and outdoor enthusiasts as part of the Reserve's goal to make sure we humans do little to no damage to the environment and cultural history.

Tangible actions to protect the Reserve are not always popular with the neighbors, and this is one of the more challenging parts of the executive director's job. Requests to put up billboards, create access easements across the property, do mowing, and add benches, picnic tables, memorial signs for loved ones, and step stools for horseback riders have been turned down, much to the disappointment of those making the requests. Permission to hold mountain bike races and treasure hunts for equestrians have been denied if the organizers don't agree to cancel the events if wet trail conditions occur. All of this can lead to very negative reactions from the residents, organizations, and the public if the reasons for denial aren't fully explained.

I did try to follow what the head of the U.S. Army Corps of Engineers office in St. Paul, Chuck Crist, said during the land transfer: "I'll try to say yes before I say no." For example, the education program gradually expanded after some proven successes and with input from student and instructor surveys and extra precautions in place. Because class fees pay for the programs and instructor contracts, the majority of the board also supported the incremental expansion of class topics, frequency, and ages served. Limits were placed as protections, such as confining any outdoor classrooms or structures to areas of previous impact, like the visitor center grounds. With the priority of safeguarding the ecological diversity and cultural history of the Reserve for the long term, it became a frequent refrain that the education program is the best method of instilling protection as a shared value via the youngsters attending the classes or field trips.

All in a Day's (and Night's) Work During a Deluge

Speaking of kids and life lessons, my worst nightmare nearly came true in 2016.

The whole day had been hot and humid. It was a relief to be working at the front desk of the visitor center for the air-conditioning. A mom and her two kids had registered to camp. It was the final week of summer vacation, and the family from Illinois wanted a remote camping experience.

I started the usual refrain that camping in the Reserve may be different than what most people are used to: "No running water or toilets; limited cell phone reception; just a flat area for tents and a fire pit." By the brand labels on their clothes and the white-on-white tennis shoes, they didn't look like they'd be comfortable roughing it. She insisted that they really wanted to do it. *Make memories before the kids became teens*, I guessed. Shade and a creek to cool off in were their only requests. So I gave them the directions to the Pott's Corner site, which features a flowing well and nearby Weister Creek. I also shared that there was a forecast for storms overnight, confirmed they would keep an eye to the sky, and pointed out the local radio stations to check for weather updates via the car radio.

The storms arrived later than expected but also packed a lot more punch. National Weather Service radar showed flash flooding for Iowa and southeast Minnesota. Following the 2007 and 2008 floods, I became somewhat obsessed with storm tracks because just a few miles north or south made a huge difference in how fast the tributaries would fill the Kickapoo River. If the Root or Turkey Rivers were flooding to the west, the Kickapoo would most likely be next.

The family of three was camping at Pott's Corner, right at the base of a steep hill next to a main tributary. Around ten thirty that night, I called the sheriff's department and asked them to have an officer do a welfare check at the site. The dispatcher said they already had roads underwater on the western side of the county. They wouldn't do a welfare check but instead insisted that they would evacuate the group and bring them to meet me at the visitor center, where they could stay out of harm's way overnight.

I took my husband's truck for higher clearance, as it was raining so hard that I didn't know if my car would make it. The creek bordering our land was high but not threatening. I remember thinking I'd overreacted. Maybe the worst would miss us to the south.

When I arrived at the visitor center, I was surprised to see three squad cars already there. As the officer had the Illinois family follow him to safety, he met one of the canoe livery owners in a full-size shuttle bus who wanted to drive down the Old 131 Trail in the Reserve as there was a group of fifteen kids and two counselors at a riverside campsite. The site is adjacent to a former roadbed that became a recreation trail and was, therefore, closed to vehicle traffic. The officer radioed for assistance, and another officer brought him the key to the trail gate as the rain continued.

After getting the drenched family of three settled in the visitor center's library, I checked the calendars and reservation binder to confirm that we had no group listed. The livery owner had not registered the group now in need of evacuation with us. The staff and I had no idea they were there.

Turns out that it was a group from Madison. They were from a reputable nature center that offered multiple trips for kids throughout the summer, but we hadn't heard from them this summer. I would later find out that the canoe livery owner told them he'd work out the camping with the Reserve if they rented from him. That would be an issue for later, as the rain somehow seemed to be pouring down even harder. No raindrops, just sheets of water.

The officers got through the gate and found the kids and counselors. The college-age counselors had no idea where they were or what was happening. Officers indicated that they could hear the force of the river water raging and the snapping of logs and limbs as the water continued to rise. They loaded the canoe livery bus and headed out but had to head south because the river had risen over the trail they'd come in on. We were listening and participating in the conversation over the scanner: officers telling the bus driver to follow them, me relaying that I hoped Bridge 13 wasn't already underwater because it was their only route out and that the next-best option would be to hike them uphill and wait it out. By some miracle, the bridge was passable, and they arrived at the visitor center.

The kids and counselors were scared and drenched but safe. It was almost two o'clock in the morning, and the front desk landline phones started ringing. I'm not sure how parents heard about the flooding, but they were calling the only location name they had on the camp itinerary to check on their kids. The tears flowed as the kids heard their mom's or dad's voice. As a parent myself, I couldn't imagine what that must have been like. Tragedy was narrowly averted as the Kickapoo River demonstrated its ability to flood in a flash.

The news headlines on August 25, 2016, focused on the Iowa flash flood that caused one fatality: an older man tragically swept away in his vehicle when he tried to drive through flood water. Mentally, I wrote my own headline: "Seventeen Young People Very Lucky to Be Alive."

I've often wondered if the family from Illinois ever went camping in a remote area again.

The Flood of Déjà Vu

As the scientific study through UW-Madison showed in 1974, municipal wastewater, private septic systems, and manure runoff from farms would have to be controlled to maintain even a base level of water quality had the dam been built. Every time I float down the river, it startles me to see that a large amount of sediment from upstream, which has been deposited on the banks of the Kickapoo since the 1800s, is still visible and vulnerable to the next high-water event.

More current data from a citizen monitoring program on the Kickapoo River and the Weister Creek project reveal the presence and dramatic increases of *E. coli*, phosphorus, and nitrogen in the watershed after snowmelt or rainfall. More frequent and heavier rainfall events overwhelm small village sewage treatment plants that are permitted to discharge when conditions warrant. Liquid manure injections, barnyard runoff, and spreading of biosolids on agriculture fields exacerbate the problem.

Weather events dumping four to eight inches of rain in a matter of hours create so much force through the area's narrow valleys that everything in the river and tributary corridors is inundated with floodwater. The force of the water clearly illustrates that there is no man-made structure big enough or strong enough to control the river system. Following the back-to-back floods of 2007 and 2008, my mantra for the most cost-effective and achievable response to flooding became "stay out of the river's way."

However, I had to rethink this belief when fifteen inches of rain fell in less than twenty hours in August 2018. As the torrential storm tracked along the northern rim of the Kickapoo Valley that day, floodwaters rushed down the valley so hard and so fast that there was very little time to get out of the way. Residents of the small town of Coon Valley had to be evacuated from hillside homes, not because they were adjacent to Coon Creek but because each hillside developed roaring rivers that wiped out homes, roads, and barns. Multiple small dams throughout the watershed failed due to the increased water pressure. The village of Ontario, just north of the Reserve, had barely enough time to get their people to safety. The town square, businesses, homes, and nearby farms will never be the same because of the significant damage. One Ontario resident, whose home is well out of the floodplain, tells the story of the force of the water pushing his door in with such pressure that the door whacked him in the head. Throughout the overnight flood, he could hear the neighbor's cows bawling as they struggled with the force of the water.

The village of La Farge, just south of the Reserve, had a little more warning as they heard the reports of what was happening throughout the upper reaches of the watershed. Evacuations were successful, but the electrical substation was inundated with water and had to be shut down. Residents were without electricity for three days in some cases, which caused emergencies for those dependent on oxygen and other medical services. Roads were blocked in every direction for hours.

When the water finally receded, the damage was revealed. Huge segments of highway blacktop were picked up by the force of the water and deposited elsewhere. Culverts were gone, as were guardrails and signage. Flood mud was everywhere, and its unique smell is something none of us who worked in it will ever forget. It was a miracle no humans died in this devastating flood.

The KVR Visitor Center did not lose power, and we opened the doors to anyone who needed to charge devices or just have a place to hang out and make phone calls. State officials checked in with us and offered assistance. I remember a specific phone call with the deputy secretary of the Department of Administration, who asked how they could help. I suggested they could get fuel to the area so the town and county patrolmen could gas up the plow trucks pushing the mud off the roads because the gas stations in each village along the river were inundated and couldn't sell floodwater-contaminated fuel. "The water got into the fuel tanks?" he asked in shock. Yes, the water got in everywhere.

As the communities within the Kickapoo Valley embark on post-flood recovery planning and flood resiliency measures for the future, the discussion isn't limited to getting out of the way of the river. Since the floodwaters exceeded previous high-water marks, both residents and businesses outside of the floodplain are adopting flood-resistant practices. Some businesses will replace wood floors with concrete ones, which are easier to hose down after a flood. Residents contemplating building new homes are considering living without a basement, and a consortium of communities is considering funding an alarm system that uses gauges and remote cameras to alert residents and visitors during a flash flood.

A wonderful project captured many of the stories of those directly impacted by the 2018 flood. "Stories from the Flood" recorded thorough accounts of area residents and the municipalities that endured the flood. A collaborative effort through the Driftless Writing Center, the Wisconsin Humanities Council, and students from both UW–Madison and La Crosse, the collection is archived and available online and as a book through the UW–La Crosse Oral History Project. The coordinators did a great service by letting the people tell their stories, which helped many people work through the trauma from the flood. Once completed, evening events were held throughout the area to share the stories, video, and book that resulted from the project. I highly recommend it as further reading to get a true sense of the physical, mental, and fiscal impacts from the disaster.

Climate change is clearly impacting the Kickapoo Valley. Our "new normal" includes heavy rainfalls in short periods of time and above-average temperatures in winter with sudden thaws that create ice jams and overflows at culverts, tributaries, and the river. I recall only one year during my tenure when we had to warn campers to be extra cautious with campfires due to dry conditions, while we had to issue warnings about flash flooding nearly every year and sometimes multiple times per season. Following the historic flooding of 2018, the shallow water table and soils were so saturated that an otherwise normal rainfall of a couple of inches caused the Kickapoo to exceed its banks quickly.

The Wisconsin Priority Watershed Program of the 1980s and '90s was a wonderful model to address nonpoint sources of pollution, such as soil erosion and nutrient runoff from farm fields. At-risk watersheds received additional funding for county conservation departments to work with landowners and farmers on the implementation of practices to reduce runoff. Contour strips with alternating crops slowed the water as it flowed downhill, and buffer strips along stream banks helped filter sedimentation before it hit the water course. The financial incentives worked, but once the funding was cut, many practices were abandoned.

Current regulation of nonpoint pollution is limited to large-scale farms or for voluntary conservation programs in Wisconsin. Clearly, there are a variety of factors landowners and farmers consider when it comes to managing their land. Crop farmers face fluctuating prices and yields every season. Farmers trying to utilize every strip of what little available productive farmland they have for cropping and grazing is understandable but can be problematic for the floodplain and river.

The problems of flooding and erosion are old ones in the Kickapoo Valley, as previously noted. A July 1972 newsletter from the Wisconsin Botanical Club quoted the 1970 U.S. Geological Survey that stated, "The Kickapoo Watershed has one of the 4 or 5 highest erosion rates in Wisconsin, estimating soil losses of at least 100–400 tons per square mile per year...[and] soil loss of over 100,000 tons per year at La Farge."[15]

Fast-forward forty years to the previously referenced Weister Creek habitat project on the western edge of the Reserve, where wholistic restoration practices have demonstrated success in reducing erosion rates. Jeff Hastings of Trout Unlimited and Paul Hayes, a former KRMB member and project liaison, made a joint presentation on the success of the Weister Creek project at a field day event. Jeff told the attendees:

> Before starting the project, we determined that 80 percent of the sediment getting into the creek was coming from bank erosion. This means that water quality is a huge part of our restoration projects. Pulling the banks back on a gentle slope is key to making the banks stable and helping to mitigate the impacts of flooding on the watershed.[16]

Over the years, practices have evolved to include addressing the steep, erodible banks in addition to the filtering from buffer strips.

Resiliency has become the current buzzword in discussions about long-term flood recovery. How can government programs help our residents, infrastructure, businesses, and homes become more resilient during these major rain events? Doing this will take a regional approach with attention paid to upland practices as well as streambank practices. Evaluating where wetlands have been lost and comparing the abilities of deep-rooted prairie plants and woodlands to hold up during extreme storms are being promoted for research studies. Determining how to reconnect the hydrology of springs to tributaries and then to river systems and prioritizing where work will

---

15 James H. Zimmerman, "The La Farge Dam," Wisconsin Botanical Club newsletter, July 1972, WiBotanicalClubNewsletter and USGS Survey, https://pubs.usgs.gov/ha/376/plate-1.pdf.

16 Reporter Gillian Pomplun of *SW News*, a weekly newspaper, attended the presentation and cited the comment, https://www.swnews4u.com/local/environment/trout-fishing-and-flood-resilience-are-improved-restoration-efforts/.

have the biggest benefit are also on the list.

Questions about whether changes in infrastructure practices have made the water run off faster need to be answered as well. For example, the Wisconsin DOT and local highway departments need to evaluate whether the installation of larger but fewer culverts has inadvertently concentrated the flow into fragile ravines that allow the water to pick up speed, power, and tons of sediment as it heads toward main channels. In conjunction, policymakers and the Federal Emergency Management Agency need to change their requirement of funding the replacement of structures "to their preflood condition" without considering design improvements that could prevent repeated replacements in the next flood.

Stabilizing the uplands so they absorb more of the rainfall will require cooperation from farmers and recreational landowners. Wisconsin is losing farmers at an alarming rate, and many of those who remain have converted to more efficient and technologically advanced practices. As one local farmer says, no-till farming saves soil, oil, and toil because it reduces trips across the field, and avoiding soil loss is one of the major goals of current conservation plans. However, when one of these significant rain events happens, the no-till ground may not absorb water as well as tilled soil can. In addition, the contour and buffer strips are sometimes removed from fields to accommodate larger equipment. Smaller-scale organic farming and rotational grazing have been touted as solutions, but both come with their share of problems too. Small farms don't guarantee conservation practices, and the fencing required for rotational grazing of pastures is tough to maintain when it gets washed out repeatedly by high-water events on even the smallest of tributaries.

In short, everything needs to be on the table. The tributaries and main stem of the Kickapoo River are going to continue to do what they do: fluctuate, meander, and impact the landscape. Planning for resiliency means rethinking where people and businesses are located and offering them a safer place to go while providing them with good reasons to move. Putting a dollar figure on proposed changes may help earn support, as it is clearly more cost-effective to invest in increasing upland stability rather than frequently repairing downstream devastation.

Whatever the future holds, the KVR, with its 8,600 acres, is well suited to be one small part of the overall solution. And even with all its challenges, the unique management structure and commitment to protecting this beautiful river and property offer great hope for long-lasting success for this Driftless paradise.

Epilogue

In 2019, I started giving serious thought to my exit strategy as executive director of the Kickapoo Valley Reserve. I had worked full-time since college graduation in 1988, and I was planning to use my cache of sabbatical hours to enjoy some extended time off. This was fun to think about, and I felt fortunate that the KVR was in the best shape it had ever been. The board members and the staff were actively committed to their roles. The budget was stable, and the number of people visiting and loving the property and programs was continuing to grow.

I announced my intentions to the board and staff so they'd have time to prepare. I planned to parallel the position and work alongside whoever was selected for a few months before stepping down.

Then the pandemic hit. The visitor center was closed to the public, but the trails and river were busier than ever. People felt safer outside, but the new-to-the-outdoors visitors weren't as adept at navigating a secluded place, and they expected some services. Since the pandemic limited staffing to essential positions only, I was back out in the field more than I'd been in years.

The education program and all special events were suspended due to the pandemic, and therefore, no revenue was being generated other than trail and camping passes. Daily decisions about what could and couldn't be allowed were exhausting, even though they were relatively minor compared to what other people were facing globally. As everyone knows, the whole darn year was unbelievably stressful and bizarre. I was one of the fortunate people to still have a job. But from my perspective, I felt like the job was finished; the land was protected, education programs were expanding, and recreation was increasing. I needed a new challenge to re-energize and motivate me.

Just prior to the pandemic, I had received a call from Governor Tony Evers's deputy chief of staff, asking if I'd be interested in serving on the Natural Resources Board (NRB), a seven-member citizens' board responsible for advising and setting policy for the DNR. I would be filling a vacancy, and even though I would have to go through state senate approval, I was eligible to start serving immediately. I was honored to be asked and civic-minded enough to know that you don't say no to the governor.

The NRB appointment opened my eyes to many of the major issues facing Wisconsin. Natural resource topics are near and dear to my heart, but the increasing political divisiveness in the state and the impact of the pandemic got me thinking about doing something more.

In February 2021, I was notified that the Wisconsin Economic Development Corporation (WEDC) was seeking candidates for the position of director for the Office of Rural Prosperity. I had always thought that "rural prosperity" was a bit of an oxymoron, but I remembered seeing the *Voices for Rural Prosperity* report in an email earlier in the year. It was a product of the governor's Blue Ribbon Commission on Rural Prosperity. Normally, I am of the mindset that a commission report is just a diversion that lets politicians say they're studying an issue, but it just ends up collecting dust on a shelf somewhere. However, this report seemed different, given the variety of ideas that came out of it and the unique mix of people who worked on it.

My friend and fellow rabble-rouser Luke Zahm encouraged me to apply when I mentioned it to him. As fellow political junkies, he and I would banter nonstop about the "state of the state." After being told that I was one of three finalists, I was forced to think about whether I was serious about taking the job. I was really looking forward to getting the KVR reopened and operational post-pandemic, then riding off into the sunset at the end of the year with a complete pension and in good health.

On Saturday, March 6, 2021, I had just settled onto the couch after dinner when I received a call from the Vernon County Sheriff's Office, saying that a hiker was reported missing on the Reserve. They couldn't get in touch with our officer, and they wondered if I would come and unlock the gates so they could expand the search. I immediately headed to the Reserve, even though we had donated bolt cutters to all the area emergency services with instructions to cut the chains if they ever needed access for an emergency. By ten o'clock that night, nearly a hundred local volunteer firefighters, area police officers, and emergency medical technicians were on the scene to start the search, aided by several trained drone operators. Fortunately, the hiker was found with the help of a drone and all those dedicated souls.

As I stood outside the maintenance building, with the ambulance and fire truck lights flashing, my mind leaped ahead to what we had all imagined would be bad news. The temperature had dropped to nineteen degrees, and the hiker had already been out on the trails for at least seven hours. When she was found safe and sound, the young woman refused medical treatment and didn't seem to grasp the gravity of her situation and how many people were out looking for her. I can only hope that someday she will realize how incredibly lucky she was.

That night I decided I would take the job at the WEDC if it was offered to me. I didn't have the energy to get through another busy summer dealing with the public while managing the Reserve. I submitted my official resignation on April 1, 2021, with an end date of Earth Day on April 22 and a promise to assist as much as I could with the exhibit upgrade and the process of finding the next executive director. Increasing the workload of executive assistant Erica Cronk and education coordinator Jonel Kiesau was my greatest regret. But I knew that between them, the KVR, the new charter school planning, and the outdoor classroom construction were in good hands.

Looking back, I feel this was the right decision at the right time. The NRB position fills my need to work on environmental issues, and being the director of the Office of Rural Prosperity provided an opportunity for me to learn new things and help improve the quality of life in Wisconsin while remaining a neighbor and frequent visitor to the Reserve.

My first paddle that spring was on Billings Creek, from Highway F at the north edge of the Reserve, on to the Kickapoo River for a few miles, and exiting at Landing 10. I had never paddled Billings Creek before, and I'm hesitant to report that it was beautiful out of fear that if the wrong people learn about it, they'll ruin it. The early spring ephemerals, faster spring current, and enough riffles to make me pay attention were energizing and beautiful. It all visually reaffirmed that the water will just keep doing what it did long before we got here and will flow long after we're gone.

The river knows; we'll get there someday.

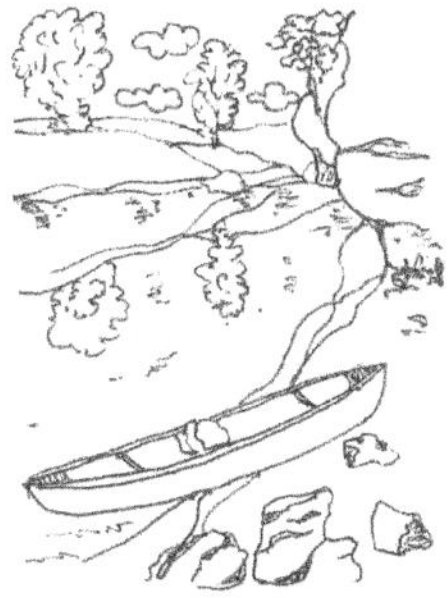

Appendix

Memorandum of Understanding & Joint Management Plan for the Kickapoo valley Reserve

MEMORANDUM OF UNDERSTANDING
between
the Ho-Chunk Nation and the State of Wisconsin

WHEREAS, the WATER RESOURCES DEVELOPMENT ACT OF 1996, §361 provides for the decommissioning of the Kickapoo River Flood Control Project and for the transfer of lands, acquired by the federal government to facilitate the creation of a reservoir, to the Ho-Chunk Nation and the State of Wisconsin [hereinafter State] on the condition that the State and the Ho-Chunk Nation [hereinafter Nation] have agreed and entered into a Memorandum of Understanding containing certain provisions required by the ACT, by October 31, 1997;

WHEREAS, the Kickapoo Reserve Management Board [hereinafter Board] and the Nation propose to jointly manage the 8,569 acre tract of land commonly referred to as the Kickapoo Valley Reserve [hereinafter Reserve] in Vernon County, Wisconsin, having a land description of Section 31, Township 14 North, Range 1 West of the 4th Principal Meridian; Sections 2 through 11, and 16, 17, 20, and 21, Township 13 North, Range 2 West of the 4th Principal Meridian; and Sections 15, 16, 21 through 24, 26, 27, 31, and 33 through 36, Township 14 North, Range 2 West of the 4th Principal Meridian;

WHEREAS, the Board was created and empowered by Wisconsin State Legislative Act 349 Laws of 1993 to manage and exercise jurisdiction over those state lands commonly known as the Reserve. The Board is authorized by the same state legislation to promulgate rules and regulations for the protection, conservation, and maintenance of state owned land in the Reserve in its natural state, which strictly prohibits the Board from selling the land or allowing mining of any sort within the Reserve;

WHEREAS, the Nation, a federally recognized Indian Tribe vested with the inherent powers traditionally associated with and vested in sovereign nations, organized under and pursuant to 25 U.S.C. 476, through its legislative enactments exercises its inherent right to manage, control, and conserve those lands deemed part of the Nation reservation or trust lands;

NOW THEREFORE, the State and the Nation based upon their mutual promises and consideration agree, in conformance with the requirements of the WATER RESOURCES DEVELOPMENT ACT OF 1996, §361, as follows:

1. The Reserve will be preserved in a natural state and developed only to the extent necessary to enhance outdoor recreational and educational opportunities.

2. The Reserve will be managed following the policies articulated in the Management Plan (Attachment 1) and administered through the Board in cooperation and consultation with the Nation. The application of the Management Plan shall be consistent on both state and tribal lands within the Reserve. The Board shall have responsibility for managing state lands and the Nation shall have responsibility for managing tribal lands within the Reserve. The

policies of both the Board and the Nation shall be consistent with the mutually agreed upon Management Plan.

3. The lands to be transferred to the Department of the Interior, in trust for the Nation are: those areas located within the Reserve identified on the attached Map A and generally encompassing portions of Sections 15, 22, 23, 26, in the township of Whitestown and those portions of Sections 4 and 9 in the township of Stark.

4. The Management Plan will be reviewed three (3) years after the transfer of lands are made to the State and to the U.S. Department of the Interior in trust for the Nation, and each fifth year thereafter at which times the State and the Nation may agree to changes to the Management Plan in order to address changed circumstances.

5. The Board acting on behalf of the State agrees to limit public disclosure of the location or existence of each site of particular cultural or religious significance to the Nation, to the extent the law allows.

6. The State shall seek legislation adding two (2) voting representatives of the Nation with expertise in archaeological and cultural resources to the Board. The Board shall seek an amendment to chapter 41, Wisconsin Statutes, providing the Board with the authority to transfer lands to the Nation consistent with the WATER RESOURCES DEVELOPMENT ACT.

7. The Board and the Nation shall develop a Memorandum of Agreement within one year of the signing of this Memorandum of Understanding, incorporating enforcement of the Reserve's policies and procedures, and addressing law enforcement concerns for the entire property to prevent desecration of archaeological, sacred and historic sites or damage to the natural environment.

8. In balance with the State responsibility, the Nation may agree to pay a sum sufficient in lieu of taxes to the local government directly affected by the placement of lands into trust located within their geographical boundary.

9. Following each review of the Management Plan conducted pursuant to Part 4 of this Memorandum of Understanding, the State, through the Board, agrees to consider future transfers of land within the Reserve to the U.S. Department of the Interior to be held in trust for the Nation which contain sites, discovered subsequent to the transfer of the initial 1200 acres described in Part 3 of the Memorandum of Understanding, of cultural or religious significance to the Nation. The consideration of future transfers under this section of the memorandum of Understanding shall include the following:

    a. Whether the subsequently discovered site or sites of religious or cultural significance to the Nation located on State land in the Reserve may not be adequately protected under state ownership.

b. Whether the site or sites that have been discovered, subsequent to the original transfer described in part 3 of this Memorandum of Understanding, on State lands within the Reserve are of cultural and religious significance to the Nation
c. Such other criteria that the State and Nation agree to include in the Management Plan.

It is understood that any associated lands transferred with a site or sites of religious and cultural significance to the Nation under this section of the Memorandum of Understanding shall include those lands minimally necessary to afford adequate protection of the site or sites. It is also understood by the State and the Nation that future land transfers are not guaranteed under any circumstances, but will be given fair consideration.

10. The State and the Nation jointly request that the simultaneous transfer of the entire 8,569 acres from the U.S. Army Corps of Engineers to the State and the U.S. Department of the Interior Bureau of Indian Affairs in trust for the Nation required under the Water Resources Development Act of 1996, be no later than January 1, 1999.

11. The lands to be transferred to the Department of the Interior, in trust for the Nation shall be placed in trust, pursuant to the Water Resources Development Act of 1996, at the same time title to the remaining lands of the Reserve are given to the State.

Signed this 30th day of October 1997 by:

Mr. Jacob H. LoneTree
President, Ho-Chunk Nation

Mr. Tommy G. Thompson
Governor, State of Wisconsin

JOINT MANAGEMENT PLAN

for the
KICKAPOO VALLEY RESERVE

by the
HO-CHUNK NATION AND STATE OF WISCONSIN

SUMMARY

This Management Plan sets the terms and conditions for the State of Wisconsin and Ho-Chunk Nation to preserve the Kickapoo Valley Reserve in its natural state and allow for development only to the extent necessary to enhance recreational and educational opportunities as prescribed in the enabling legislation.

The Plan provides for joint management of the Reserve by the Ho-Chunk Nation and Kickapoo Reserve Management Board on behalf of the State of Wisconsin. Through development of this plan, and in conjunction with the Memorandum of Understanding and Programmatic Agreement, both parties are agreeing to:

- protect the reserve and all it contains with special protections for its significant cultural and environmental designations;
- provide for managed public access to balance various user groups with the overriding mission to protect the Reserve;
- share the benefits of knowledge with future generations by enhancing educational opportunities through the Reserve;
- cherish the history of the reserve, its resources and the lives of the people that have been affected by political and natural occurrences which ultimately led to this project;
- mediate disputes in an orderly fashion;
- take the appropriate steps necessary to secure funding for administering the activities and maintenance of the Reserve;
- continue to work together in good faith to insure the agreements are carried through.

It is acknowledged that the Ho-Chunk Nation and Kickapoo Reserve Management Board may choose to address specific issues on their respective acreage differently. This is accepted by both parties with the understanding that the methods to address those issues do not lose sight of the overriding commitment to protecting the Reserve.

JOINT MANAGEMENT PLAN
FOR THE
KICKAPOO VALLEY RESERVE

INTRODUCTION

The Water Resources Development Act of 1996, §361 provides for the transfer of lands acquired by the federal government for the Kickapoo River Flood Control Project to the Ho-Chunk Nation, to be held in trust by the Bureau of Indian Affairs, and the State of Wisconsin. The Ho-Chunk Nation and the State of Wisconsin, acting through the Kickapoo Reserve Management Board, have agreed that the Kickapoo Valley Reserve, being of such unique value, shall be "preserved in its natural state and developed only to the extent necessary to enhance recreational and educational opportunities."

The Kickapoo Valley Reserve is an 8,569 acre tract of land located in Vernon County directly north of La Farge, Wisconsin. The Reserve extends from the northern boundary of La Farge approximately nine miles north to the southern border of Wildcat Mountain State Park, near Ontario, Wisconsin.

AUTHORIZATION

The Federal Water Resources Development Act (WRDA) of 1996 authorizes the transfer of ownership of the Reserve property from the U.S. Army Corps of Engineers to the Ho-Chunk Nation (HCN) and State of Wisconsin. Wisconsin Act 349 Laws of 1993 established the Kickapoo Reserve Management Board (KRMB) and their authority to govern the Kickapoo Valley Reserve. Article V, Section 2(I) of the Ho-Chunk Nation Constitution, grants the Ho-Chunk Nation Legislature the authority to "negotiate and enter into treaties, compacts, contracts, and agreements with other governments, organizations, or individuals."

WRDA requires that for the land to transfer ownership the following documents need to be in place by October 31, 1997:

1) A Programmatic Agreement prepared by the U.S. Army Corps of Engineers - St. Paul District and agreed to by the Bureau of Indian Affairs, the Advisory Council on Historic Preservation, the Wisconsin State Historic Preservation Office, the HCN, and KRMB in accordance with Section 106 of the National Historic Preservation Act and its implementing regulations for the protection of cultural resources.
2) A Management Plan, which includes conceptual terms and conditions for management of the lands. This document serves as and shall be incorporated in full text into the Memorandum of Understanding.
3) A Memorandum of Understanding prepared and approved by the State of Wisconsin and HCN which includes: this Management Plan, a description of sites and associated lands going to the Secretary of Interior to be held in trust by the Bureau of Indian Affairs for the Ho-Chunk Nation, a provision for review of land holdings, and a confidentiality agreement for lands going to the Secretary of Interior.

MANAGEMENT PRINCIPLES

The resources of the Kickapoo Valley Reserve shall be managed jointly by the KRMB and the HCN to promote, preserve and enhance its unique natural, scenic and cultural features.

The management of the Reserve shall:

1. Protect the Reserve's aesthetic, cultural, scenic and wild qualities as well as the native wildlife and plant communities. Special emphasis will be placed on designated state natural areas, federal and state listed species, species of special concern and other unique biotic features.
2. Protect, conserve and maintain all significant cultural sites.
3. Provide for and manage the use and enjoyment by visitors and maintain a diversity of low-impact recreational opportunities for people of all abilities.
4. Utilize sound natural resource and agriculture management practices to improve water quality, maintain soil productivity and protect wildlife habitat.
5. Strive to operate a self-supporting project through grants, donations, bequests and fee-based recreation that are consistent with the overriding commitment to preserve the Reserve's natural features.
6. Establish and maintain a Rural Education Center which includes information on the history of Native American tribes and Euro-American habitation of the Reserve.
7. Develop and maintain a Land Use Master Plan for the Reserve which includes specific conservation management plans in the areas of: agriculture, forestry, natural areas, recreation, wildlife management, education, cultural resources, and emergency response.

MANAGEMENT POLICIES

A. Management Area Boundary

The Reserve boundary is recognized as the area registered under federal ownership through legal description, including: Section 31, Township 14 North, Range 1 West of the 4th Principal Meridian; Sections 2 through 11, and 16, 17, 20, and 21, Township 13 North, Range 2 West of the 4th Principal Meridian; Sections 15, 16, 21 through 24, 26, 27, 31, and 33 through 36, Township 14 North, Range 2 West of the 4th Principal Meridian; located entirely within Vernon County, Wisconsin.

Within that boundary the Department of Interior, Bureau of Indian Affairs holds in trust for the HCN 1,200 acres which are in portions of Sections 15, 22, 23, and 26, in the township of Whitestown and portions of Sections 4 and 9 in the township of Stark. Property remaining within the Reserve boundary and excluding the lands held in trust shall be transferred to the State of Wisconsin. Both parties recognize existing road and utility easements on the property.

In accordance with the Water Resources Development Act of 1996, §361, and the Memorandum of Understanding, upon mutual agreement during review of the Management Plan, the State of Wisconsin may transfer additional acres to the United States of any additional site(s) discovered to be culturally significant to the HCN.

B. Management Authority

The KRMB and HCN are committed to cooperatively managing the Reserve lands. To achieve this goal, the parties hereby agree to the terms and conditions established through this management agreement and the adjoining Memorandum of Understanding and Programmatic Agreement.

The State of Wisconsin through §41.41, Wis. Stats., established the KRMB, articulating the KRMB's duties and authority to act. The KRMB's membership shall consist of: four local representatives; two watershed representatives; and three at large appointments representing recreation and tourism, education, and environment; and two representatives for the HCN with cultural resource expertise (pending introduction and approval by the Wisconsin State Legislature).

Lands held in trust by the Bureau of Indian Affairs for the HCN shall be managed consistently with the Reserve lands to the extent practical. The HCN Legislature has the authority to further restrict activities or grant special permits for those lands held in trust after notifying and considering comment by the KRMB.

The KRMB shall set policy, approve a Master Plan, and be fiscally responsible for the Reserve lands held by the State as outlined in portions of chapters 15, 20, and 41, Wis. Stats. The KRMB is attached to the Wisconsin Department of Tourism. The Department is responsible for support on administrative, personnel, legal and budget issues.

C. General Land Management Policies

1. Agriculture

The KRMB will continue the practice of agriculture leases on the state-owned portions of the Reserve. The KRMB will continue to require all lessees to follow a conservation management plan. Pesticide restrictions will continue in those areas identified in the Endangered Species Protection Agreement developed by the Wisconsin Department of Agriculture, Trade and Consumer Protection and U.S. Army Corps of Engineers. A detailed Agriculture Management Plan assessing soil suitability, productivity, bid process and impacts on natural areas and cultural resources will be completed during the preparation of the Master Plan for the Reserve.

2. Forestry

The Kickapoo Valley Reserve contains a treasure in forestry resources. That treasure includes types and ages of trees that need the utmost protection, poorly managed cultivated forests that need selective harvesting, as well as areas in need of reforestation. Logging and harvesting of timber primarily for commercial purposes are prohibited on all Reserve lands.

To properly manage the forest resources, a Forest Management Plan will be included in the overall Master Plan. The Plan will inventory the resources; identify areas and methods for protecting and maintaining a healthy forest system within the Reserve; and make recommendations for appropriate restoration of oak savannas, prairies or other native forest habitats.

3. Natural Areas

Significant tracts of natural areas exist within the Reserve. The Wisconsin Department of Natural Resources has identified the areas meeting the legislatively defined criteria as Natural Areas in §23.27, Wis. Stats, within the Reserve. In addition, the Reserve is listed federally as a National Natural Landmark through the U.S. National Park Service. In the event any portion of the Reserve transfers ownership, a conservation easement is placed on Natural Area lands for protection through perpetuity.

A Natural Areas Management Plan will be included in the Master Plan to meet the obligation set by having these designations and ensure protection of the unique characteristics that make up the Natural Areas.

D. Recreation Management and Facilities Development

A Recreation Management Plan will be developed for inclusion in the Master Plan in the spring of 1998. The Recreation Plan will provide details on camping, trail use and maintenance, map of accessible locations, registration, a visitor's "Outdoor Code of Ethics" describing proper procedures (litter control, noise, etc.), and user fees. Following are policy recommendations to be incorporated into the Plan:

1. Camping

Low-impact campsites are appropriate in the Reserve. Low-impact is defined as those campsites which have minimal impact or intrusion upon the natural environment and ecosystems. Physical permanent structures are prohibited. Temporary tents or camping equipment that do not require permanent fixed features or support are included as an example of possible low-impact campsites. The development of campgrounds shall be prohibited within the Reserve. Small, minimal impact sites serve to highlight the geographical features of the Reserve while minimizing the environmental impact. Sites that have to be traveled to by foot or other non-motorized means will be included. User fees will be established by the KRMB. All visitors will be required to follow a "pack-it-in, pack-it-out" rule for litter control. It is the position of the KRMB and HCN that there are areas within the Reserve that are so culturally and environmentally significant that no camping will be allowed. Those areas shall be designated by the KRMB and HCN, jointly.

2. Trails

All future plans will make use of existing trails to the extent possible rather than risk causing damage by creating new trails. Where mitigation and restoration of a trail are required, the KRMB must make all accommodations necessary to avoid adverse impact on cultural sites that may be affected by the modification(s). Trail use shall be limited to pedestrian traffic, hiking, non-motorized bicycles, horseback riding, snowmobile, cross-country skiing, snow-shoeing and handicap access. Trail access will be regulated by season, time, and may be subject to rotation or restricted use to protect the quality of the designated Natural Areas. Special permits may be granted by the KRMB on State lands and the HCN on trust lands for formal and/or accredited educational instruction or training.

3. Canoeing

Bodies of water and navigable streams are recognized with special status by law. The Kickapoo River is the most densely used area in the Reserve. Impact of canoeing on the Reserve is inevitable. Litter control and waste disposal are essential to protecting the Reserve, therefore canoeists will be required to follow the same "pack-it-in, pack-it-out" policy of the Reserve. The KRMB shall designate a limited number of areas upon which it would be appropriate for canoeists to launch or exit the waterways. Such areas should be designated with consideration given to multiple purposes such as areas that have existing launches or campsites and where human impact is at a minimum on the Reserve.

4. Hunting and Gathering

The State and HCN agree to allow public hunting in the Reserve following the State hunting seasons, licensing, permits and regulations. Under §29.106, Wis. Stats., members of the HCN may be granted permission to take deer out of the state calendar season for religious feasts, funeral rights, and warrior feasts. Such permits require notification of the conservation warden by a clan leader. A separate agreement will be developed for gathering of ceremonial or medicinal plants on non-federal land. Visitors to the Reserve are allowed to gather mushrooms, wild berries, and other herbs without special permits except those species listed as endangered or threatened.

5. Fishing

State laws govern fishing on waters within the Reserve. State imposed licensing, size and bag limits will be followed and enforced.

6. Other Recreation Activities

The Reserve will encourage a wide variety of compatible activities be held on the Reserve. For example: bird watching, photography and ceremonial events are appropriate activities which may be addressed in other areas within the Master Plan. Event permits will be developed by the Board for activities including but not limited to: dog trials, special hunts, skill tests and races.

F. Cultural Resources

The Programmatic Agreement elaborates on the protection of significant cultural sites as established by the federal criteria set forth in the National Register 36 CFR sec. 60.4, 800.4, and National Register Bulletin No. 38 and the Cultural Resources Management Plan.

The Cultural Resources Management Plan will address the process to allow reasonable access for Native Americans, including members of the Ho-Chunk Nation, to cultural resources on lands transferred to the State for the purpose of practicing religious and cultural traditions. Equivalent consideration will be granted for access to cultural resources on Trust lands.

Both parties agree to notify the other and the State Historical Society of any activity on their lands which may have an adverse effect on a significant site(s). Activities that require notification include: ground disturbance, physical destruction, damage or alteration of any part of a property which would adversely affect the historic significance of that property; isolation of a property from or alteration of the character of the property's setting when that character contributes to the property's qualification as a listed property; introduction of visual, audible or atmospheric elements that are out of character with a property or alter its setting; neglect of a property resulting in its deterioration or destruction. The State Historical Society Officer will be given the opportunity to comment within thirty (30) days and afforded reasonable opportunity to perform a survey and provide a response.

Notification is not required for such activities as: re-issuance of agricultural leases which contain no significant cultural sites and maintenance of existing infrastructure including roads, trails and camp sites. Marker Trees, as defined in the Cultural Resource Management Plan, will be protected from all cutting.

Following the transfer, cultural research and surveys conducted on state owned land within the Reserve will require a permit from the State Archeologist as outlined in §44.47(2), Wis. Stats.

E. Education

Education for all ages on a variety of topics is a focal point for the Kickapoo Valley Reserve. Within five years the KRMB, in conjunction with other entities, will develop the structural blueprint, outline funding commitments, explore feasibility of location and detail cooperative arrangements for construction of a Rural Education Center.

A thorough Education Plan will be included in the Master Plan. Topics in the Education Plan should address a broad spectrum including but not limited to: cultural history, history of the La Farge Dam Project, Native American Culture, historical farming and forestry, the story of the Kickapoo River itself, the cultural diversity of the area, sustainable land use, conservation, modern agriculture, lumbering and timber management, alternative energy, living exhibits, working animals, driftless area natural history, geology, plant and animal communities, prairie restoration, native animals and the role of community based conservation.

G. Infrastructure

1. Transportation Systems

The State and Ho-Chunk Nation recognize the need for highway safety but are obviously concerned about the impact re-construction could have on the overall appearance of the Reserve in terms of noise, impact during construction, and aesthetics. Therefore, the KRMB and HCN will work closely with the Federal Highway Administration, Wisconsin Department of Transportation, and County Highway Commission to offer input on design, materials, construction methods and unique opportunities for safe, Reserve-friendly highways.

2. Law Enforcement

A separate agreement for enforcement will be established as referenced in the Memorandum of Understanding. In general, legislation authorizes enforcement by the Wisconsin Department of Natural Resources for state hunting and fishing regulations. Law enforcement on highways and roads within the Reserve will follow standard procedure by state and local police departments. Funding and staff considerations will need to be addressed in the Master Plan and annual budgets for patrolling and enforcement of visitors beyond hunting, fishing, and road traffic.

3. Emergency Response Measures

Inherent to a project of this magnitude, the need exists to plan for the worst: ·flash floods, forest fires, injured visitors or other unexpected problems. The KRMB will work with emergency response experts from local communities to write an Emergency Response Plan to be included in the Master Plan by spring of 1998.

PROHIBITED ACTIVITIES

The following acts or uses are expressly forbidden within the Reserve. There shall be no:

1.destruction or removal of cultural features or artifacts;
2. removal of natural features (exceptions for edible fruits, nuts, berries, grasses, etc.);
3. removal of rocks, minerals or similar materials;
4. litter, dumping or improper disposal of waste or hazardous materials;
5. destruction or removal of property having historic or educational purpose, unless it poses an immediate risk of danger to life and health;
6. fireworks of any kind;
7. release of dogs, cats or other pets prone to becoming feral; domestic animals in the reserve must be under command or physical control of their owner;
8. off-road vehicles used within the Reserve except when permitted or authorized by the Reserve Board for environmental, educational and cultural research;
9. parking in the Reserve, except in designated areas only.

Signs and informational pieces shall be posted within the Reserve to provide notice to all who enter of the jurisdiction upon which they have entered or crossed. Visitors to the Reserve will be informed that there exists multiple legal jurisdictions subjecting them to state, tribal and federal laws.

MEDIATION OF DISPUTES

If a dispute arises between the State of Wisconsin through the KRMB, and Bureau of Indian Affairs through the HCN, either party may refer the dispute to mediation by request made in writing to the other. Within fourteen (14) days of the receipt of such a request, the parties may each select one (1) mediator and mutually agree on the selection of a third trained and impartial mediator, who shall compose in-full a panel of three persons to preside at and over a mediation between the parties.

DEDICATION OF HUMAN AND FISCAL RESOURCES

Annual budgets and staffing plans will be prepared in January of each calendar year in preparation for request through the State and HCN's fiscal year.

A long-term financial management plan will be included in the Master Plan for the Reserve.

CONCLUSION

The State of Wisconsin and the Ho-Chunk Nation reserve unto themselves the rights not requiring further approval of the Kickapoo Reserve Management Board to engage in all uses that are permitted by governmental, state and tribal law or regulation, that do not substantially impair the conservation and preservation values of the Kickapoo Reserve or are inconsistent with the purpose of the Reserve as articulated in the Programmatic Agreement, Management Plan, Water Resources Development Act and Memorandum of Understanding. The Kickapoo Reserve Management Board, with the financial cooperation of the State, the Bureau of Indian Affairs and the Ho-Chunk Nation reserve the right to maintain and repair trails, bridges, structures, and appurtenances that are already in existence within the Reserve or may be built in the future consistent with the aforementioned documents. The Ho-Chunk Nation and the Kickapoo Reserve Management Board reserve the right to conduct and grant permission to conduct educational and non-profit activities that are consistent with the protection, conservation and preservation values stated within the Memorandum of Understanding.

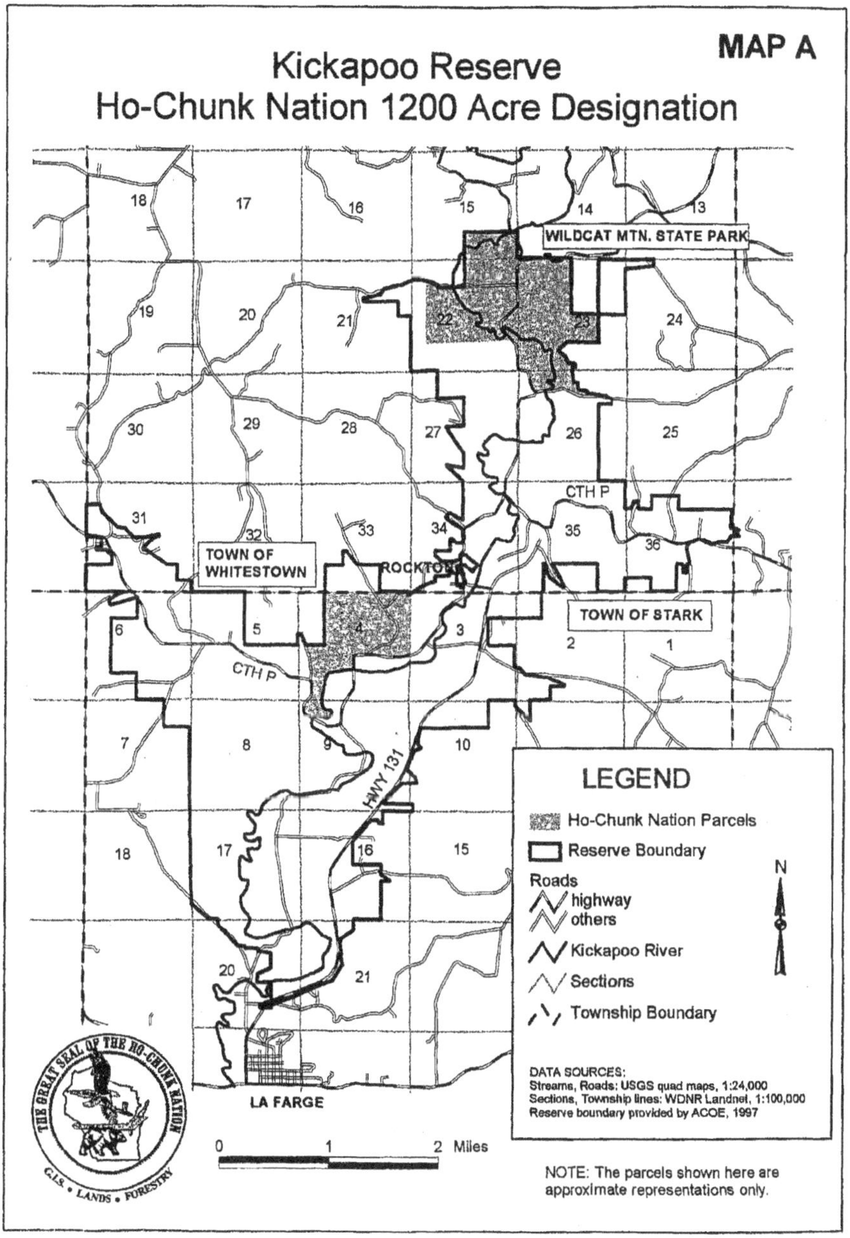
MAP A
Kickapoo Reserve
Ho-Chunk Nation 1200 Acre Designation
WILDCAT MTN. STATE PARK
TOWN OF WHITESTOWN
ROCKTON
TOWN OF STARK
CTH P
HWY 131
LA FARGE
LEGEND
Ho-Chunk Nation Parcels
Reserve Boundary
Roads
highway
others
Kickapoo River
Sections
Township Boundary
N
DATA SOURCES:
Streams, Roads: USGS quad maps, 1:24,000
Sections, Township lines: WDNR Landnet, 1:100,000
Reserve boundary provided by ACOE, 1997
0 1 2 Miles
THE GREAT SEAL OF THE HO-CHUNK NATION
G.I.S. • LANDS • FORESTRY
NOTE: The parcels shown here are approximate representations only.

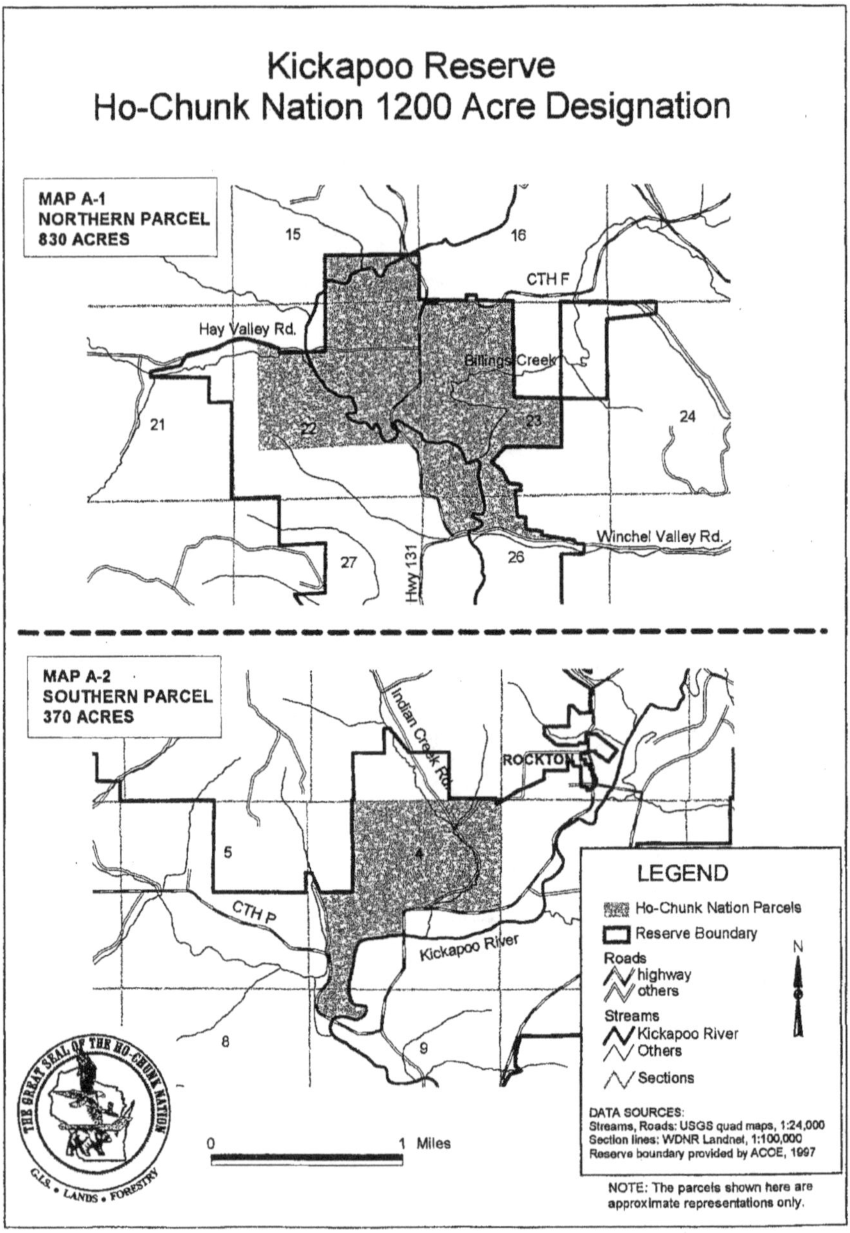

Kickapoo Reserve
Ho-Chunk Nation 1200 Acre Designation
MAP A-1
NORTHERN PARCEL
830 ACRES
15
16
CTH F
Hay Valley Rd.
Billings Creek
21
22
23
24
27
Hwy 131
26
Winchel Valley Rd.
MAP A-2
SOUTHERN PARCEL
370 ACRES
Indian Creek Rd
ROCKTON
5
4
CTH P
Kickapoo River
8
9
LEGEND
Ho-Chunk Nation Parcels
Reserve Boundary
Roads
highway
others
Streams
Kickapoo River
Others
Sections
N
DATA SOURCES:
Streams, Roads: USGS quad maps, 1:24,000
Section lines: WDNR Landnet, 1:100,000
Reserve boundary provided by ACOE, 1997
NOTE: The parcels shown here are approximate representations only.
0
1 Miles
THE GREAT SEAL OF THE HO-CHUNK NATION
G.I.S. • LANDS • FORESTRY

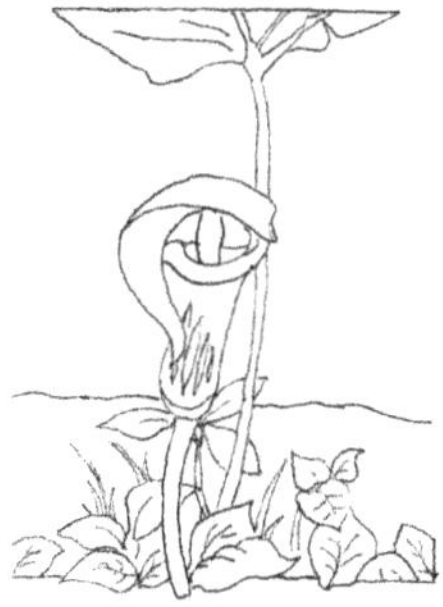

Suggested Further Reading

Books

Bartelt, Jerry, Owen Boyle, et al. *The Ecological Landscapes of Wisconsin: An Assessment of Ecological Resources and a Guide to Planning Sustainable Management*, Chapter 22, "Western Coulees and Ridges Ecological Landscape." Wisconsin: Wisconsin Department of Natural Resources, 2015.

Catton, Theodore, and Matthew Godfrey, *Steward of Headwaters, U.S. Army Corps of Engineers 1975-2000*. Minnesota: U.S. Army Corps of Engineers, St. Paul District, 2012, https://digitalcommons.unl.edu/cgi/viewcontent.cgi?article=1145&context=usarmyceomaha.

Dott, Robert H. Jr., and John W. Attig. *Roadside Geology of Wisconsin*. Montana: Mountain Press, 2004.

Heasley, Lynne. *A Thousand Pieces of Paradise: Landscape and Property in the Kickapoo Valley*. Wisconsin: University of Wisconsin Press, 2012.

Institute for Environmental Studies Center for Biotic Systems. *Environmental Analysis of the Kickapoo River Impoundment: A Report to the U.S. Army Corps of Engineers*. IES Center for Biotic Systems, November 1974.

Lewis, Philip H. *Tomorrow By Design: A Regional Design Process for Sustainability*. New York: Wiley, 1996.

Nuzum, Ralph E. *At Work in the Kickapoo Valley*. Reports and Studies via the Kickapoo Reforestation Nuzum Fund. UW–Madison College of Agriculture and Life Sciences, 1996.

Steinmetz, Brad. *La Farge: The Story of a Kickapoo River Town*. Wisconsin: Kickapoogian Press, 2010.

Steinmetz, Brad. *That Dam History: The Story of the Lafarge Dam Project*. Wisconsin: Kickapoogian Press, 2011.

Sterling, Bonnie, ed. *The People Remember...: An Oral History of the Kickapoo La Farge Dam Project*. Wisconsin: Friends of the Kickapoo Valley Reserve, 2004.

Articles

Bence, Susan. "Toxic Conditions in Wisconsin before the Clean Water Act," WUWM Public Radio, October 19, 2015. https://www.wuwm.com/podcast/wuwm-news/2015-10-19/toxic-conditions-in-wisconsin-before-the-clean-water-act

Drew, Elizabeth P. "Dam Outrage: The Story of the Army Engineers," *The Atlantic*, April 1970, https://www.theatlantic.com/magazine/archive/1970/04/dam-outrage-the-story-of-the-army-engineers/661780/.

Gatz, Laura. "Clean Water Act: A Summary of the Law," Congressional Research Service RL30030, October 18, 2016, https://crsreports.congress.gov/product/pdf/RL/RL30030.

"Kickapoo Denied Designation as Park, Waterway," *La Crosse Tribune*, June 27, 1976.

Tenenbaum, David. "'Stories from the Flood' Recount Suffering, Resilience in Kickapoo Valley Towns," UW–Madison College of Letters and Science, November 12, 2019, https://news.wisc.edu/stories-from-the-flood-recount-suffering-resilience-in-kickapoo-valley-towns/.

Acknowledgments

Thank you, Dave West. Your love, support, and patience over our many years together are amazing. Love and hugs to Andie and Keegan for putting up with your mom's job, late-night meetings, and *all that nature stuff* from your childhood to adulthood.

With gratitude to my siblings, bonus siblings, nieces, and nephews. Thanks for raising me right.

Everyone may have a story to tell, but putting it down in a format people may want to read was harder than I could've ever imagined. From start to finish, a number of people guided me or simply said, "You can do it." Thank you, David Hough, for your incredible guidance, advice, and wisdom. This would never have gotten finished without you and Loma Huh's masterful copy editing it into print worthiness. And my emotional support team: Karen Brandl ("you get one exclamation point in life"), Jonel Kiesau, Tamara Dean, Caroline Gottschalk-Druschke, Andrew Savagian, and Sandra Dee Naas.

To all the board members who served as citizen volunteers including; Ron Johnson (aka Boss), Rebecca Zahm, Don Coleman, Sandy Heidel, George Nettum, Jack Robinson, Cathy Onsager, Dave Kluesner, Susan Cushing, Sharon Folcey, Gail Frie, Randy Heisel, Tamara Riddle, Richard Lowe, Dick Wallin, Bill Quackenbush, Jo Deen Lowe, Senn Brown, Katie Thompson, Tracy Littlejohn, Jim Moe, Dawn Makes-Strong-Move, Brandon Hysel, Tina Brown, Bill Greendeer, Al Szepi, Paul Hayes, AJ Mann, Reggie Nelson, Dave Maxwell, Julie Hoel and Travis Downing. You've left your mark on this place, and I am eternally grateful for your dedication.

Staff members throughout the twenty-four years who shared my hopes in protecting this special place. Your work made it a reality. Cheers!

To the leaders, members—past, present, and future—and donors to the Friends of Kickapoo Valley Reserve; your shared appreciation, devotion to volunteering, and financial support are vital to making the KVR what it is.

The Kickapoo Valley has its share of icons. A few I came to know and appreciate for always setting me straight include Dean Hamilton, David and Kay Mick, Brad Steinmetz, and Chuck Hatfield.

Equally iconic are Henry Peterson and Orville Jensen, who have been informing the UW Foundation and Kickapoo Reforestation/Nuzum Fund administrators about the Kickapoo Valley and ensuring the Wisconsin Idea made it to the valley for years. Speaking of educators, thank you, Paul Robbins—*just write it* (ha!), Adena Rissman, the Kickapoo Reforestation/Nuzum Fund panel and administrators, the UW Writing Center, Driftless Writing Center, and Little Creek Press.

Eric Epstein, I owe you and Craig Thompson a truckload of Cheetos for everything you two taught me through the years. Mike Lutz, the nicest attorney I've ever met, thank you for sharing your notes and memories. Ben Johnston, Erica Cronk, and Ben Ewing are the unsung masters who complete "all other duties as assigned."

Oh, how I wish some of my departed friends and advisors were here to see how it all came together: James Daines, Mary Bufton, Phyllis Gabrielson, Maxine Shird, Bernice Schroeder, Rod Nilsestuen, Karen Parker, John Blackdeer, Rex Whitegull, Bill Kelbel, Mark Patronsky, Andy Gorrill, Mom and Dad.

Protecting Paradise is dedicated to the elected officials and public employees who put partisanship aside to get something done. Special thanks to Al Anderson, Senator Feingold, Mary Jo Repko, Governor Tommy Thompson, 3rd District Congressmen Steve Gundersen and Ron Kind, Brian Rude, DuWayne Johnsrud, Jennifer Shilling, and Lee Nerison.

Pį̨nagigi wi̜ną to the Ho-Chunk Nation leaders and staff willing to take a chance on this unique arrangement. I have fond memories of stories shared by Anna Rae Funmaker, Marlon WhiteEagle, Chloris

Lowe (Sr. and Jr.), Willard Lonetree, Orville Greendeer, Jon Greendeer, Ritchie Brown, and Dallas Whitewing.

Congratulations to the people of the Kickapoo Valley. You have protected an incredible piece of *paradise*!

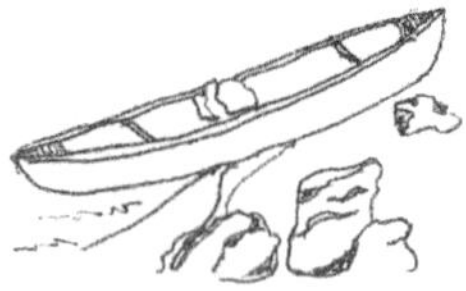

About the Author

Marcy West served as the Executive Director for the Kickapoo Reserve Management Board (KRMB) from 1996-2021. Born and raised in Wisconsin she has had a lifelong appreciation for environmental issues. Earning a degree in Natural Resource Management through the University of Wisconsin-Stevens Point, her career always involved protecting the resources and allowed her to never stop exploring the rivers, lakes and forests. She and her husband reside in the Kickapoo Valley and manage their own piece of paradise for pollinators, wildlife and solitude.

INDEX

A

B

C

D

E

G

H

L

M

N

O

S

U

V

W

Z

www.ingramcontent.com/pod-product-compliance
Lightning Source LLC
LaVergne TN
LVHW050547310125
802592LV00003B/346